HEGEL'S
PHILOSOPHY OF RIGHT

Continuum Reader's Guides

Aristotle's Nicomachean Ethics – Christopher Warne

Heidegger's Being and Time – William Blattner

Hobbes' Leviathan – Laurie Bagby

Hume's Enquiry Concerning Human Understanding – Alan Bailey and Dan O'Brien

Nietzsche's Genealogy of Morals – Daniel Conway

Plato's Republic – Luke Purshouse

Mill's On Liberty – Geoffrey Scarre

Hume's Dialogues Concerning Natural Religion – Andrew Pyle

Wittgenstein's Tractatus Logico-Philosophicus – Roger M.White

HEGEL'S
PHILOSOPHY OF RIGHT
A Reader's Guide

DAVID ROSE

continuum

Continuum International Publishing Group
The Tower Building   80 Maiden Lane
11 York Road   Suite 704
London SE1 7NX   New York, NY 10038

British Library Cataloguing-in-Publication Data
A catalogue record for this book is available from the British Library.

The author and publisher thank Cambridge University Press
for permission to reprint from: Hegel, G.W.F.,
Elements of the Philosophy of Right, trans. Nisbet, H., and ed. Wood, A.,
© Cambridge University Press, 1991.

'A Chinese man stands alone to block a line of tanks heading east on
Beijing's Cangan Blvd. in Tiananmen.' © AP/EMPICS.

ISBN: HB: 0-8264-8710-6   9780826487100
PB: 0-8264-8711-4   9780826487117

Library of Congress Cataloguing-in-Publication Data
A catalog record for this book is available from the Library of Congress.

Typeset by Servis Filmsetting Ltd, Manchester
Printed and bound in Great Britain by MPG Books Ltd, Bodmin, Cornwall

To Laura and Nicholas, with all my love.

CONTENTS

ACKNOWLEDGEMENTS

It is common practice to acknowledge people rather than events, but this book has been as much moulded by the birth of a son, changing institution, decorating a new home and travelling backwards and forwards on the sprightly new trains of GNER and Virgin as well as the Cold War-inspired carriages of Transpennine railways. More sincerely, I am grateful to the authors of the books and articles I have read and the papers I have heard over the years who should find themselves mentioned in the bibliography. I should also mention Dudley Knowles whose fault it was that I ever properly read Hegel in the first place and to thank him for guiding me through the tricky process of understanding the subject matter. Also, Sarah Douglas and Adam Green at Continuum Books who accepted every delay with an optimistic rescheduling.

A great debt of thanks to my parents, Bert and Eileen, who supported me through the long years of study and now have something tangible to show for it.

Finally, and most importantly, all my love to Laura, who has always been there for me, pushing and prodding when needed to get me to where I am now. Oh, and to Ugo, without whom this work may have been vastly different.

ABBREVIATIONS TO THE WORKS OF HEGEL

Citations will either be by page number or paragraph (§); 'R' refers to a remark and 'A' to an addition. Unless followed by an abbreviation, they refer to: *Elements of the Philosophy of Right*, trans. Nisbet, H. ed. Wood, A., Cambridge: Cambridge University Press, 1991. Other citations from the works of Hegel will be indicated by the following abbreviations:

EL   *The Encyclopaedia Logic: Part 1 of the Encyclopaedia of Philosophical Sciences with the Zusätze*

EG   *Philosophy of Mind: Part 3 of the Encyclopaedia of Philosophical Sciences with the Zusätze*

FPR   *Lectures on Natural Right and Political Science: The First Philosophy of Right*

JR1   *System of Ethical Life and First Philosophy of Spirit*

NL   *On the Scientific Ways of Treating Natural Law, on its Place in Moral Philosophy, and its Relation to the Positive Sciences of Right*

PhG   *The Phenomenology of Spirit*

SL   *The Science of Logic*

SS   *System of Ethical Life and First Philosophy of Spirit*

VPG *Philosophy of History*

CHAPTER 1

CONTEXT: A TALE OF TWO REVOLUTIONS

Hegel lived in interesting times. Whether this was a blessing or a curse, it was no doubt integral to the formation of both the man and his thought. Culturally and politically, Europe was being swept into uncharted waters by the criss-crossing wakes of the two great revolutions: the political one originating in France and the industrial one spawned by England. As these movements led to the migrations of people and urbanisation, giving birth to war and a drive to Empire, they began to undermine and modify the old social order of Europe. And Hegel lived such times interestingly. He inhabited a Germany that had risen to the forefront of philosophical inquiry and he was, legendarily, to be found finishing and dispatching his first masterpiece as the Napoleonic armies (much to his then support) bore down on Jena. He lived through the French Revolution, its subsequent Terror, the progressive Prussian reforms and the eventual reinstatement of a weakened political status quo. His philosophy began with an optimistic hope in the possibility of a reformed political and religious order before maturing, like the man himself, into a conservative, yet critical, endorsement of the post-Napoleonic social landscape.

Georg Wilhelm Friedrich Hegel was born in Stuttgart on August 27, 1770 to a middle-class family, his father being a civil servant at a provincial court. He encountered philosophy at the gymnasium (secondary school), but his intellectual stimulation would have been at its height in the period from 1788 to 1793 when, attending a seminary for Lutheran pastors in Tübingen, he shared a residence with the poet Hölderlin and the philosopher Schelling. Many of the themes that were later to recur in his philosophy were no doubt the fruit of heated debate between these three intellectuals: the admiration for a supposed Athenian Golden Age, the ideals of social and national unity and the reformation of religion. There was also an initial enthusiasm for the events in France of 1789; the young men celebrated the revolutionary spirit they expected to reinvigorate Europe.

The French Revolution made a political reality of the predominant theory of the time. Of the many differences between social contract thinkers, they were united by the claim that society was an association of individuals for the benefit of those individuals. Implicit to this movement was the rejection of the claims of the *ancien régime* that society was a natural or divine order justified by the qualitative difference between types of men. Instead the declaration of equality amongst men was, firstly, expressed in the Reformation and its denial of the qualitative duality between the priesthood and the laity, and then politically in the English Civil War and the Glorious Revolution of the seventeenth century before culminating in the destructive drive for egalitarianism and individual worth of revolutionary France. The development of this concept, so thoroughly modern, promised – so it seemed to Hegel and his friends at the time – the possibility of a political rationalisation of outdated social institutions.

Of course, such initial hope turned to dismay when the centrifugal force of the revolution became, in the Terror, an arbitrary and senseless assertion of the power of individual wills and abstract ideals. Hegel's conception of modern subjectivity, both its positive and negative aspects, was in so many ways an expression of the mini historical narrative from the Reformation to industrialisation, and his ethical and political thought remained directly concerned with the balancing of a subjective need for expression and a social need for unity. The evils of the revolution and, to an equal extent, the industrialisation of Europe could be seen in the atomisation of modern society and the rise of the legitimacy of individual expression against objective standards of value. The narrative itself was to form the focal point of his first complete monograph, the *Phenomenology of Spirit*.

Hegel's academic career started slowly. He began as a tutor in Switzerland and Frankfurt, before following his younger and more successful friend Schelling to Jena, who had already secured a professorship. Hegel used his inheritance to subsidise his unsalaried position as a *Privatdozent* – a teaching assistant – and published his first major works: *The Difference between Fichte's and Schelling's*

System of Philosophy (1801) and *The Scientific Ways of Treating Natural Law* (1802), the latter being a critical reading of atomistic approaches to ethical and political thought and containing a critique of Kantian moral philosophy. More significantly, in 1807, he published the inconsistent but astonishing account of the philosophical development of both the individual and the species, in *The Phenomenology of Spirit*. At the heart of the work is the recognition of the need for reconciliation between the human mind and nature (in its broadest sense); a reconciliation that – in this early work – he claimed would be attained through religion and philosophy, but would later, in the *Philosophy of Right*, shift in focus to an ethical and political resolution.

The disruptions caused by the Napoleonic defeat of Prussia at Jena forced Hegel to move away in 1807, and for a while he took the post of an editor of a newspaper, before becoming a rector of a gymnasium in 1809. His remit was to implement a radical reform of education with his speculative method of philosophy at its heart. He was also able to produce the *Science of Logic* (the first volume in 1812 and the second in 1816), and, if his students were encouraged and able to read these volumes, there would be no argument against the assertion of falling standards in education.

The achievement of his first paid university post came when he was appointed in Heidelberg in 1816. It was from this period on that Hegel began to publish his lecture notes, *Encyclopaedia of the Philosophical Sciences*, in order to aid his students through his dense and demanding lectures, which were later to be revised and expanded into three volumes: on logic, nature and spirit. He also delivered his first lectures on the idea of right and political philosophy, and he reached the pinnacle of his academic fame when he was invited to fill the vacant Chair of Philosophy in Berlin, last occupied by Fichte.

In Berlin, Hegel prepared his lecture notes on political philosophy for publication but hesitated as historical events once more affected the nature of political power. The progressive nature of Prussian politics since the defeat of 1806 had slowly returned to a weakened, reactionary aristocracy. Reform had been halted after the final defeat of Napoleon in 1815 and was fuelled by an establishment paranoia about the rise of anarchy and the revolutionary spirit amongst the people, a fire stoked by the assassination of a reactionary playwright by the student Karl Sands. Universities were seen as cultivating an environment of radical thought and subversive action and many of Hegel's friends and academic rivals found themselves prohibited from university posts. Professors could find themselves dismissed, as Fries did, who Hegel unwisely attacked in his preface to the *Philosophy of Right* for encouraging revolutionary attitudes.

It was in this context that the final version of lecture notes for the *Philosophy of Right* were published in 1821 and Hegel found himself elected to Rector of the university in 1829. He died on November 14, 1831.

Hegel had lived through the apex of Enlightenment thought and, unlike his predecessor Kant, perhaps had a glimpse of its limitations and dangers. As we shall see, he celebrates modern subjectivity as the pinnacle of human history, yet is acutely aware of its atomistic danger to society and its subjectivist danger to truth. Whereas the Enlightenment encouraged all humans to reason for themselves and to legitimise all dictates of authority, society and others through the use of free and public reason, Hegel fervently believed that such subjectivity was one-sided. The individual cannot decide what is true and right on his or her own, but must have standards of legitimacy against which to validate his or her assertions. His very un-enlightenment stand was to seek reconciliation in the social world of interpersonal subjectivity and not in universal and free reason. Whether or not it is accurate to describe Hegel as a man of the Enlightenment is controversial. He thought reason had to be sovereign, but saw it as an historical development and not a given; he wanted the state to be rational, but critically rejected the social contract insights into political authority; he thought freedom to be the highest good, but saw a perfectionist social world as liberation.

CHAPTER 2

OVERVIEW: HEGEL'S *PHILOSOPHY OF RIGHT*

AMBITION OF THE GUIDE

This book does exactly what it says on the tin. It is a reader's guide to Hegel's *Philosophy of Right* and it does not aspire to be anything more than that. In the following pages, I shall endeavour to present Hegel's ideas as he himself develops them in the sections of the *Philosophy of Right* and in relation to the context of both his ideas as a whole and the time in which he was writing. If reading philosophy is much like climbing a mountain, then Hegel would probably be K2. Introductory books ought to work like crampons, as necessary props to ensure that a reader who approaches the primary text for the first time does not fall to the ground or – as is more common – have a poke at the cliff and decide to scale it another week. But, one also needs a base camp and this is the best role I can envisage for the current work. There are more comprehensive interpretations, but they are almost as daunting to approach as Hegel's own work. My aim is to supply confidence for the reader to approach the text him or herself and then go on to these other introductions. Such a confession of humility, though, ought to be tempered with further confessions of more serious academic sins.

It is not only the intention of this book that limits its ambition but also its size. To reduce Hegel's own condensed lecture notes into more manageable and accessible prose when the previous one hundred and seventy years have been spent enlarging them seems counter-intuitive at best. Yet, the length of this volume is, paradoxically, both its strength and its weakness. The philosophical thought of Hegel is notoriously obscure and involved and many would think it impossible to summarise the richness of the *Philosophy of Right* into less than two hundred pages, yet the restriction has made me approach writing this introduction more as if I were designing a map with a viable (but not exclusive) route up the mountain, than offering an interpretative and comprehensive reading. And this is a strength because there is already material which requires robust philosophical training that can be used as crampons later on when the confidence of the reader is assured.

But, the restriction to less than two hundred pages is also a weakness, motivating me to make some controversial editorial decisions. Put simply, certain themes and issues had to be passed over or touched on only briefly. This is most clearly the case in the discussions of the third part of Hegel's work which concerns the actual structure of the constitution and the social arrangements of the state. I have chosen to concentrate on the groundwork – the theory – that justifies Hegel's state and, hence, have spent far more time on the first two parts and on the concept of ethical life. I have done so in good conscience, since I believe once the reader has the requisite understanding in place, the discussions of the family, civil society and the state itself will be comprehensible and familiar as they concern subjects which we all engage with on a day-to-day basis.

More significantly, one writes with an ideal of one's reader fixed as an image before one's eyes. My ideal would be the mature student who is taking a combined honours course or an evening class and wishes to understand Hegel as part of the context of European political or philosophical thought. I would be surprised if the *Philosophy of Right* was the first work in philosophy or political science that he or she has ever read and I assume my reader approaches this book with basic knowledge of the ethical thought of modernity (Hobbes, Locke, Rousseau and Kant), although this is not absolutely necessary. For this reason, I happily make reference to such ideas (and explain where I believe it necessary), but I play down the role of metaphysics in the argument. Metaphysics is a taxing discipline and one that requires a thorough grounding in the basics before any discussion can begin. Hegelian metaphysics is notoriously opaque and obfuscating and although a full understanding of the *Philosophy of Right* would require a digression into its location in the system of Hegel's philosophy as a whole, I am strongly of the opinion that much of his lecture series does not require it. Hegel is discussing why human beings live in association with other human beings and what this means for both the individual and the state. He talks about freedom, action, right and wrong, the family, private property and the structure of the constitution. We can all say something about these issues and what Hegel has to say is often clear and reasonable. The full justification of why we ought to accept the grounding claims of Hegel's political philosophy (that one cannot radically critique one's existing society, or that Northern Europe is the necessary end of the development of human spirit) does require an understanding of the metaphysical system that contextualises them, but as the first step on a journey to comprehension, one can be permitted to merely hint at what form such a justification would take without having to digress beyond the limits of the text itself. I simultaneously play down the notorious jargon of Hegel's own lectures, avoiding the very strong temptation to spend pages explaining the use of neologisms and terms of art which Hegel utilises with perpetual indiscretion. Instead, I opt for a language more conducive to our own times. I believe Hegel's ideas in the realm of ethics and politics can be explained without recourse to a 'specialist' or 'technical' language, and this is a belief reinforced by Hegel's own remarks and additions (see below) to his lecture notes, where his style metamorphoses into the lecturer reinforcing a point and then the teacher who uses contemporary issues and examples to illustrate more clearly.

Furthermore, the *Philosophy of Right* is still caught in a quagmire of controversy concerning Hegel's own – authentic, as it were – position. Is he a conservative with an eye on reform? Is his model of the political state authoritarian? Much of the secondary literature is concerned with supporting one or other of these positions. I try to be neutral in my approach, to present the text as one would read it naively and innocently. Such controversies will no doubt engage the reader after they have reached a certain level of understanding, but I think it best to reach that understanding without prejudice. Yet, to hold my approach to be silent on these concerns would be disingenuous; if no scientist is value-free, then it would be foolish in the extreme to assume nothing of my own personal reading of Hegel appears in the following pages. We all have prejudices and perspectives and so, to be honest and transparent, I must acknowledge that I read Hegel as a rational conservative who advocates reform when required, but views any attempt to rationally reconstruct the state according to the determinations and demands of pure reason or universal moral realism as a nonsensical and dangerous undertaking. This puts him clearly between two camps: those who view Hegel as a reactionary concerned with ingratiating himself to the powers who be; and those who read in Hegel's obscure metaphysical approach a more radical and far-reaching critique of his contemporary social world.[1]

Yet, to add a proviso to all these worries, the reader ought to view this book only as the beginning of an expedition. It is a modern misconception that information and knowledge ought to be immediate; we rarely read a book more than once or delve too deeply into the context or background that gave rise to it, instead assuming that the words on the page themselves – if read at the correct pace – will disclose all their truth. This is sadly not true and, above all, certainly not in philosophy. Understanding becomes fuller and more robust with re-reading and reinforcement and the shortfalls of the approach I have decided to take will be slightly compensated by the indications in the further reading section. The reader, once confident enough, should begin the climb proper.

HOW TO READ THE BOOK

Given what has been said above, and the current climate whereby we find instructions on the side of shampoos on how to use them, perhaps I ought to say a little about how I believe this book ought to be read. First, it is important that a copy of the *Philosophy of Right* is close at hand. Ideally, I would urge the reader to read the relevant section of Hegel's *Philosophy of Right* (for example, the Preface), then the relevant chapter here (Chapter 3) before re-reading Hegel himself. In this manner, the reader will bring his own understanding to the text, be introduced to what I believe is significant and return to the text to see whether he or she agrees with my reading.

I should also mention a bit about the style I have used. I am at times irreverent and often not as careful in my expression as is demanded by philosophical enquiry. I also integrate my own examples with those of Hegel's, but attentiveness to the primary text will be enough for the reader to separate mine from his. The reason for these choices is obvious: I want this introduction to be accessible and the equivalent of a lecture series on Hegel's political thought given to students. It would make little sense to have one's readers puzzling over what I say as well as Hegel's own words and so the informal style is an attempt to allow the main and taxing thought to be concerned with Hegel himself. My aim is to make myself invisible.

OVERVIEW OF THEMES

Hegel's *Philosophy of Right* is the perfect text with which any newcomer to the thought of Hegel ought to engage. Not only is it one of the classics of Western political theory and one of the most accessible of Hegel's works, but it also represents the maturation of his system of philosophy into its most rational and clearly expressed form, whilst still containing many conspicuous elements from the earlier romantic aspect of his thought. The text is first and foremost a work of normative political theory: it attempts to justify how the institutions and laws of the state ought to be structured and arranged in order for the state to be rational. For Hegel, the rational state is one in which the human can enjoy full freedom, and he introduces this central concept of his work and explains how he will extrapolate a theory of a political state from a common understanding of this notion.

The content of this book mostly follows Hegel's own structure and the titles of the chapters are direct references to his own sections, but a brief overview of the whole structure would not be amiss. The Preface, for all its inconsistencies and problems, is concerned with how one ought to (or, more accurately, should not) undertake political philosophy. It both introduces, in brief, the aims of Hegel's lecture series and offers a taste of how he will carry his enquiry out. The introduction is where the real work begins as it presents the main normative elements of Hegel's theory (freedom and rationality) and anticipates how they will be developed in the succeeding pages. The next parts of his work are developments of the basic foundations put into place in his introduction and the significance of it ought never to be underestimated. The first part on abstract right develops an account of free personality and offers an interesting explanation of the modern preoccupation with individual rights. The second part is concerned with morality and the limitations of the paradigmatic subjective standard of modern ethics, demonstrating why the subject needs an objective framework to make judgements about what is good and right. The third part supplies the understanding of how such an objective framework is appropriated from one's own tradition (ethical life) and from those institutions that determine the hierarchy and the respective force of our goods and rights: the family, civil society and the political state proper. As I have already intimated, the outline of the institutions of ethical life as Hegel conceives of them will be very generally dealt with since it is my belief that if one grasps the meaning and theory of the first parts of the book, the 'nitty gritty' of the political science in the third part becomes easy to understand since it deals with subjects with which we are all familiar.

Now with all these caveats in place, let's begin. But be careful where you walk; the path is narrow and fraught with intellectual dangers.

A NOTE ON THE TEXT

If you open up your copy of the *Philosophy of Right*, you will see that nearly every section (after the Preface) is divided into three parts: the main lecture point (normal text), an indented remark and a paragraph in a smaller font introduced as an 'Addition'. Originally, the text of the *Philosophy of Right* was sold to Hegel's own students to accompany his own lecture series and included only the main paragraph and the remarks which Hegel added as elucidation of the main point. The additions were later added by Hegel's pupil Eduard Gans, who compiled them from the notes of two students, Hotho and Griesheim, who attended the lectures series at different times. The compilation of the text raises problems about authority and, as a rule, the main paragraph and remark ought to be trusted more than the addition since Hegel had no control over the publication of these, but in this book I have made no qualitative difference between Hegel's own text and the additions. I feel vindicated due to the introductory nature of this work and also due to the long association these additions have had with the main text itself (originally appearing in 1840).

CHAPTER 3

THE PREFACE: THE TASK OF PHILOSOPHY

THE PLACE TO START

It might be thought a peculiar question to ask where exactly to start our journey through the *Philosophy of Right*. Peculiar because the expected answer would be at the beginning; this is after all an introduction to the reading of the text. However, I was indecisive about whether to discuss the preface at the beginning or at the end of this book. Such indecision arose from the fact that Hegel's preface is, at times, ironic and disingenuous: charitably, one could say it is aimed at wrong-footing the censor of the Prussian state; uncharitably one could say it is written to ingratiate Hegel with the powers that be for his own personal advancement. And he cannot resist pointed, personal, swipes at academic rivals (Pinkard, 2000, chap. 10). Moreover, the preface would have been the last part of the published notes completed and often not only alludes to the arguments and positions that follow in the text itself, but overtly assumes the reader to be aware of them. More significantly, most normal readers initially ignore prefaces to books and only return to them if the work demands or merits it.

And it was the last consideration which finally convinced me to discuss the preface at the beginning of this book since it is all too easy for the reader to ignore what is substantially interesting among all the parochial politics and contemporary necessities. So why is the preface of philosophical interest? In terms of content, it is an odd discussion of method in that Hegel does not discuss his own method explicitly but does spend adequate textual focus on how *not* to engage in the philosophy of right or what would now be termed political philosophy.[1] In a slight concession to my original worry about the actual placing of a discussion of the preface, we shall augment our reading of the preface with a brief, interwoven consideration of the first four paragraphs of the introduction and also draw in some background features of Hegel's philosophy as a whole in order to clarify later discussions.

HOW NOT TO DO POLITICAL PHILOSOPHY

Let us begin with a question: is the *Philosophy of Right* a work of normative political philosophy? Normative political philosophy ordinarily does not merely describe what the central values, institutions and practices of an actually existing state are (as political science or sociology may do), but it prescribes what they ought to be. Such a normative commitment allows us to make judgements such as 'The society that has an institution of slavery is illegitimate because it does not express and openly violates the value of equality', or 'The ban on smoking in public places is an unjust limitation of liberty', and to be able to *rationally* discuss them utilising the normal tools of definition, classification and inference. So, political philosophy can make judgements about whether such and such a society is a good society, or whether such and such an institution, policy or law is valid or legitimate and these discussions will be resolved rationally so long as the moral groundwork which advocates the central agreed values (in our examples, the values of *liberty* and *equality*) has been done.

To openly state that Hegel is engaged in political philosophy rather than political science is contentious since, for him, there is no clear distinction between the two disciplines. The normative nature of political philosophy is problematic for Hegel for many varied reasons which will be revealed through this book as a whole, but it is clear that in isolating his own 'speculative method' from other modes of cognition and, simultaneously, contrasting what he calls 'understanding' with 'comprehension', he is at odds with the naively optimistic view of the critical power of philosophy:

> To comprehend *what is* is the task of philosophy, for *what is* is reason. As far as the individual is concerned, each individual is in any case *a child of his time*; thus philosophy, too, is *its own time comprehended in thoughts*. It is just as foolish to imagine that any philosophy can transcend its contemporary world as that an individual can overleap his own time or leap over Rhodes. (21–22)

The above quotation seems, on the surface, to suggest that philosophy cannot break free from the concepts, beliefs and values of its own time and make an appeal to some objective, transcendent and ahistorical standard of right and good. So, is Hegel engaged in political science or political philosophy; that is, are his lectures a mere description of the institutions, practices and laws of the state in nineteenth-century Prussia, or are they an attempt to evaluate these institutions, practices and laws? I firmly believe the latter to be the case, but not in the way which we nowadays ordinarily understand. For us, the practical consequences of normative critique are protest or resistance embodied in claims of justice and fairness. Hegel's normative stance dismisses the idea of an external point of view, a commitment to some form of justice or fairness independent of and separate from the actual determinations of justice and fairness within the state. The 'understanding' is inadequate because it offers only the *what* and *how* of the matter. It can give us a definition of a judicial system within a state and also a description of how such a judicial system functions and executes its judgements, but the understanding as a way of knowing cannot offer us a full explanation of the concept of a judicial system let alone some external standard (or definition) of justice which can be brought to bear on our actual practices. Philosophy is neither the discovery of truth nor the taxonomy of correct concepts. Such intellectual pursuits are, for Hegel, superficial and merely descriptive:

The *truth* concerning *right, ethics, and the state* is at any rate *as old* as its *exposition and promulgations* in *public laws* and *in public morality and religion*. What more does the truth require, inasmuch as the thinking mind is not content to possess it in this proximate manner? What it needs is to be *comprehended* as well; so that the content which is already rational in itself may also gain a rational form and thereby appear justified to free thinking. For such thinking does not stop at what is *given*, whether the latter is supported by the external positive authority of the state or of mutual agreement amongst human beings, or by the authority of inner feeling and the heart and by the testimony of the spirit which immediately concurs with this, but starts out from itself and thereby demands to know itself as united in its innermost being with the truth. (11)

So, the truth of right is what is, as a matter of fact, given by the dictates of government, religion and customary morality. One error of the understanding is to conflate what is the case within one state with what is rational in and for itself since the understanding's truth is only proximate: we know it intuitively or justify it through an appeal to the code of laws of a particular state or the commands of a particular religion, or through an intuitive grasp or a feeling that it is right. In claiming that the institution of slavery in unjust, we appeal to the value of equality, yet equality is justified to members of a Christian tradition in a way that it may well not be to members of a Hindu tradition which still holds to some form of metaphysical inequality amongst human beings. And it is in virtue of one's membership in a specific tradition, rather than any robust moral realism, that gives the value its immediate appeal. None of these methods of justification can lead to comprehension of a particular law until its true ground can be articulated, that is (and Hegel has Kant and the spirit of the Enlightenment in mind even if he constantly disparages both him and it as a celebration of the 'understanding') the pursuit of the rationalisation of laws and institutions. We need to demonstrate that equality is justified not just because it has arisen from a particular history or tradition, but because it will necessarily arise from all socio-historical processes.

Rational legitimation for Kant is the demand that a law can be justified to each and every person it affects and this justification would normally be a moral one. Why should one be punished for stealing? Because, at base, one recognises that theft is an action which treats the person from whom you steal as a means to an end and therefore violates his or her autonomy. Autonomy and its test, the categorical imperative, are universal and objective standards which gauge the legitimacy of laws and institutions. However, Hegel – unlike Kant and the majority of the men of the Enlightenment – did not think that rational legitimation could be independent of and separate from the standards and requirements implicit in a given society and its institutions. There is no transcendent, universal right and justice such as the requirements of the categorical imperative. The problem with the understanding is not only that it is appropriate only for description, it is inadequate and dangerous for evaluation: if the subject must legitimate a law according to external standards free from a social context, where are such conditions to come from? Hegel believes it is the vanity of subjective opinion which becomes the lever of critique in the understanding and, as such, legitimation amounts to nothing more than the expression of mere preferences: 'the concepts of truth and the laws of ethics are reduced to mere opinions and subjective convictions' (19); I like this law, I don't like that law. But this will lead to conflict: you say x and I say not-x. Who is right? We need an objective way to decide and objectivity in this sense is what Hegel refers to as the 'gain' of 'a rational form'.[2]

So, what is the exact difference between understanding and comprehending and does the latter enable one to make evaluative judgements equivalent to if different from the standard objective account of rational legitimation? Let us illustrate this with an example. A scientific explanation of the planets will involve a *what* (a definition of what constitutes a planet) and a *how* (the laws which determine their behaviour), and this is perfectly adequate if one wishes to describe an object and its behaviour. However, when we look at a novel we can take the same approach: a what (a novel is to be distinguished from works of non-fiction and poetry) and a how (the genre, the laws of that genre and the structural requirements), yet – for all the protestations of certain critics – the full explanation of a novel will only be articulated when we make reference to the will (the intentions) which brought it about. Why was the novel written? What did the author want to express? How did the background beliefs, values and concepts of his or her time affect the imaginative production of the work? The novel, one can say, is the objective expression of the author's will.

For Hegel, the objectification of the will also happens at the level of society in its laws, institutions and structures. If a law is the imposition of a will or intention to make one act in a certain way, then we need to ask: why does someone want to make me act thus whether or not I think it is right or just for them to make me act thus? The law tells me to wear a seatbelt and I will be punished if I do not, but why should I? Laws and institutions for Hegel are externalised and solidified expressions of will. So a full explanation must involve the answer to the questions *whose will?* and *why this action?* In order to offer a full explanation we need to augment the scientific questions of what and how – the questions of the understanding – with the further questions of who and why – those of comprehension. The difference between understanding the conventions of driving a car and comprehending them are knowledge of the rules (drive on the left, indicate before turning, etc.) as opposed to an endorsement of those rules. There is a story to be told about how these rules and conventions came about and why they ought to be the way they are. Some of this story will be trivial (in the UK we drive on the left since we were never subject to Napoleonic law) and some significant (it is rational to codify traffic conventions since order benefits individuals). Free thinking is rational legitimation and a rejection of the unreflective, given nature of certain conventions and rules: I do not obey them because they are given, I obey them because I find myself *at home* in them, I see they are rational and also part of what it is to be rational in the society in which I live. But, and this is how Hegel differs from standard Enlightenment thinking, these laws and norms are *given* and not theoretically constructed or imposed by the will of individuals. The understanding can offer us metaphysical accounts of the value of liberty and equality and then it can ask whether or not this society fits the ideal or not, but Hegel believes that something which has come about due to historical progress has come about for a reason and the imposition of constructed notions of utopias is dangerous and wilful.

We ought to be careful and not overstate this. The understanding gives us 'oughts' since it offers a radical critique, 'People do behave like this, but they really *ought* to behave like that' or 'Political society is arranged thus, but it *ought* to be arranged so', and justifies such judgements through very intricate theoretical systems. Comprehension seems incapable of this since the only standard of right is found in a particular history and culture.

THE POSITIVE NORMATIVE METHOD: THE IDEA OF RIGHT (§§1–3)

In his remark to §2, Hegel outlines two mistaken ways to discuss the philosophy of right: one, *formally*, that is the attempt to deduce right from the meaning of words and the logical connections between definitions; and two, through '*facts of consciousness*' or what we might contemporarily call intuitions, in the sense that, 'I have the strong intuition/feeling that it is wrong to x'. Both are one-sided: the former is akin to building castles in the air, in that we can all deduce perfectly coherent political systems if the presuppositions and axioms which ground them are true, but their validity rests on the truth of these axioms, something which cannot be known until such systems are turned into actually existing institutions. The latter relies too much on contingency. Imagine the case of human sacrifice. I assume most of my readers are appalled by the very idea but, as this quotation about the famous conquistador illustrates, if we make an appeal to our sense of right and wrong, we do no more than assert our own preferences or cultural values:

> According to all reports, it was Cortés himself, perhaps yielding to a subconscious impulse to justify his own deeds, who first attempted to convert Moctezuma. The emperor politely heard out the Spaniard's harangue. When the great conquistador invidiously compared the pure and simple rite of the Catholic Mass with the hideous Aztec practice of human sacrifice, however, Moctezuma put in a word. It was much less revolting to him, he explained, to sacrifice human beings than it was to eat the flesh and blood of God himself. We do not know whether Cortés was quite able to counter this dialectic. (Ceram, 2001, 337–338)

Stated simply, intuitions are not universal, but expressions of our individual, social and historical characters and are – as such – arbitrary, or true merely by luck. The method that makes 'our own heart and enthusiasm' the criterion for the rationality of political institutions, moral values and laws is bound to fail.

If the preface is focused on showing above all how not to engage in political philosophy, the first four paragraphs of the introduction are an extremely succinct exposition of the speculative method. Hegel refers the audience to his system as a whole, but I shall not assume knowledge of it nor digress into it, unless absolutely necessary. We are immediately told on opening the pages of this book that the subject-matter of lectures on the philosophy of right is the Idea of right: 'The subject-matter of *the philosophical system of right* is the *Idea of right* – the concept of right and its actualization' (§1). Hegel begins his lectures by separating the term 'Idea' [*Idee*] from 'concept' [*Begriff*] and in so doing expresses his implicit absolute idealist position: an Idea is an actualisation or substantiation of a concept. In an earlier version of his lectures, Hegel is somewhat clearer about what he means here: 'Natural right has as its object the rational determinations of right and the actualization of this its idea' (FPR, §1). A concept, for him, is an abstraction from particulars, such as the concept 'green' from a collection of green objects, which is the mind's apprehension of something, but such a thing is an Idea when it is expressed and coincides with an existence. The former is a theoretical exercise of the understanding, but the latter is the union of theoretical considerations with what is actually the case. An Idea is 'the reason within an object' or the abstracted concept which rationally ought to exist (§2).

So, now we are a little clearer on what Hegel means by an Idea, we can perhaps ask what the specific Idea of right may be. The Idea of right is both a description of the concept of right and also the actualisation of these laws. The concept of right is, for Hegel, wider than the notion of law; it is a list of those principles, laws, values, orders, customs, conventions, mores and institutions which regulate the behaviour of individuals in society. It is constituted by the actual norms of a society that regulate behaviour and it covers all those instances which can be answered by the enquiry whether it was right or not to have done what one did. And there are diverse forms of right: legal, moral and conventional. It is wrong to steal, wrong to break promises and wrong not to allow those inside a train to disembark prior to boarding.

The Idea of right, then, has a positive sense in that it is an actually existing collection of social norms which regulate and determine the behaviour of individuals within a given community. The positive science of right is concerned to state what is right and legal, that is, the particular determination of law within a specific community, but such an enterprise would amount to a sociology or a history: 'The correctness of the definition [of right] is then made to depend on its agreement with prevailing ideas' (§2R). Such an exercise does not exhaust the meaning of right because if that was all it amounted to we would be left with an uncomfortable positivism: such and such a law is right because it is enacted by the relevant authority and is consistent with values of a specific society. The *philosophy* of right should not just *explain* the existence of particular laws, but *justify* them; that is, demonstrate that certain laws and mores have a necessity independent of their particular historical coming into being: '*Positive right* is in general that right which has validity in a particular state and must therefore be respected as an authority that is maintained by coercion or fear or by confidence and faith, but that can also be upheld through rational insight' (FPR, §1R). We have seen that Moctzeuma was consistent in his appeal to norms and values within his culture to explain the reasons behind ritual human sacrifice, but justification should not stop there. Hegel is well aware of the spectre of relativism haunting his approach and he evades it by an appeal to reason: right is both what exists and what ought to exist. He is engaged in normative political philosophy: when he asserts that right needs to be rational or that we are concerned with the 'necessity of the thing' what he means is that such and such a convention ought to be embodied in the social and moral fabric of the *rational* state and that such and such a social practice ought never to form part of the *rational* state (§2R). So, the realm of right – that is the laws, institutions, mores and conventions of a specific culture – is an historical development, but any particular instance of right can be justified only in terms of being either the progress towards or the fulfilment of the *rational* state. The concept of right cannot exist in abstraction like the concept of an irrational number in mathematics: it must find suitable expression in existence and exist over time, and it has to play a role in the actions of individual members of the community.

Therefore, the philosophy of right is also the description of the actualisation of these shapes of right, that is their coming-to-be or historical creation that, in some sense, justifies their current existence. Man's mode of understanding the world, those values he uses to prescribe what one ought to do and say, are always – for Hegel – historically bound. There is no universal reason, only the reason that expresses the man of pastoral communities, the man of the Middle Ages, and of the Enlightenment. Primitive man, when he states this is mine and you should not touch it, or extracts retribution for a crime, is already expressing right in an undeveloped and non-sophisticated form. It is Hegel's belief in progress that allows him to evade the charge of relativism. However, I can tell a story about how a particular law came about, but that does nothing to justify it. Take, for example, the bye-law in certain English towns (if it is in fact true) that one can shoot a Welshman carrying a longbow after dusk. There is an historical explanation of this law (that England and Wales were once at war), but such a story does nothing to justify the continued existence of the law. Telling a story about how something came about can never amount to a justification of why it exists:

> When a historical justification confuses an origin in external factors with an origin in the concept, it unconsciously achieves the opposite of what it intends. If it can be shown that the origin of an institution was entirely expedient and necessary under the specific

circumstances of the time, the requirements of the historical view-point are fulfilled. But if this is supposed to amount to a general justification of the thing itself, the result is precisely the opposite; for since the original circumstances are no longer present, the insti-tution has thereby lost its meaning and its right. (30)

However, if Hegel can show that a system of private property, for example, is a more rational distribution of goods than a system of common property, and also that for a system of private property to exist, a society has to first pass through an historical stage of common property, then he can offer a justification of the institution. And this justification rests on the notion of progress. But how do we know we are progressing? How do we know which society is at the forefront of history and which lags behind? Hegel believes he has an answer to these questions: he exists at the end of history. The end of history thesis is crucial to the full justification of Hegel's normative claims since, if he is not at the end of history, then it might be that he is unable to comprehend exactly what is rational since it is not yet actual. The thesis itself holds that self-consciousness progresses by reaching its own limits and this progress is at an end when self-consciousness knows everything. Hegel believes the notion of right is also at an end and has become fully rational in his contemporary Prussian state. Only because right is fully actualised, that is devel-oped and expressed in its rational form, can we state that what actu-ally exists ought to exist and judge other societies and past epochs as steps on the way to such an end. Of course, such a thesis is con-tentious, but we must wait to the end of the lecture series for its full explanation and justification.

Right, to return to easier pastures, is valid both formally and in terms of its content. Formally a law is valid if it has been enacted by the proper institution and is recognised as such by the people who obey it. So, in a theocratic state, a law is valid if it is the proper expression of God's will (and is enacted by the proper theological authority); in a democracy, it is valid if it is enacted by the legisla-tive branch of government. However, the formal validity of a law or right tells us nothing about its rationality, that is whether its content is valid and gives us a mere positivist account of law as detailed above. Hegel first tells us that the content of positive right is constrained by three conditions (§3). One, it is part of an intelligible historical development, that is, it does not appear untested and undeveloped, imposed on the world by the power of the will of men. Laws need to take account of human needs, geographical factors and historical influences and the nature of a particular people; they cannot be a priori constructions of pure reason. Two, and following on from one, a law is valid if it can be applied to particular cases in a specific culture without giving rise to a dysfunctional social system. The notion of responsibility, for example, that was inherent in the Greek world that determined Oedipus to be responsible for the actions of his father may have made theoretical sense, but it could not be fully rational. Such a notion of responsibility could not be embodied into a substantial account of obligations and punishment (children would have to serve prison sentences for their parents). It just wouldn't work, so – as Hegel observes – such notions of responsibility are modified by the emergence of personal responsibility under Roman law and then develop into our modern-day account of the individual person responsible for his or her own actions. Third, a law is valid if it is determinate in the decision-making process of individual members of the state. Any law that prohibited smoking, but which was ignored or not enforced and did not feature in the consciousness of individuals, is just not a law. These three features confer on the content of right a justification that upholds it through rational insight. The social world is actualised freedom: the institutions which express most appropriately rational behaviour are actualisations of the will of a rational man.

THE IMPOSSIBILITY OF RADICAL CRITIQUE

However, the problem of legitimation remains. A law is 'rational' if (i) it is meaningful within and part of an historically continuous tradition; (ii) it is socially efficacious; and (iii) it plays a role in the practical reason of citizens of the state. There is nothing, seemingly, in these conditions that rules out relativity. Kant's account of legitimation is attractive because there exists an external, objective standard of rationality which does not depend on historically contingent or culturally contextual factors; that is, the categorical imperative. Liberalism has always seen the individual's reason or desires as the measure of the legitimacy of law: from Hobbes's rational naturalism and the idea of the strongest desire, through Kant's categorical imperative and the requirements of publicity, reciprocity and universality, to the Rawlsian device of the original position. An ideal position of rationality accessible to the individual was seen as the locus of legitimacy (Hobbes, 1982; Kant, 1997; Rawls, 1972). Hegel, in these terms, belongs to a very different tradition, one that holds that the standards of rationality are internal and not external to a society.[3] Hegel is adamant that – and this becomes clearer and clearer throughout his lecture series, as do the reasons why – individual practical reason cannot be the arbiter of legitimacy.

Hegel, however, wants to integrate reason into the heart of his conservatism (the description of the actual political state of affairs and the assumption that there are good reasons that it has developed into its current structure) with the demand that the actual state of affairs must meet the requirements of reason, and it is clear that 'understanding' cannot do this. The task of the philosopher is not to tell us how to behave, oddly we already know that, but he should show how the ways in which we behave (those institutions, rules and practices which determine our behaviour) are 'rational'. The assumption, the conservative one, is that these practices are, in fact, rational but, if they weren't, could we know?

Does this mean that Hegel denies any capacity on the part of the individual to make evaluative judgements concerning the dictates of his state? Am I not able to protest and resist when the state does something that I find immoral? Rational interrogation is an attempt to appeal to external standards of rationality which Hegel seems to think do not exist. And he has a point. The attempt to appeal to universal desires – everyone wants happiness – is futile because it is empty. I want happiness and you want happiness, but for me it is rearing guinea pigs, for you it is torturing them. Is Hegel, then, guilty of conservatism or relativism? What exactly would the problem be? Well, imagine a society that practises ritual child sacrifice. Wouldn't we want to say that it is a *bad* society? However, if rational values are grounded in the fabric of the society, how can one criticise a society which is not one's own?

One possible defence is that Hegel is being disingenuous. He wants the censor to think his comments apply to the glory of the Prussian state. This is too easy and too sycophantic an answer, much of the text and the ground of his position commit Hegel to a form of conservatism. We need to ask how Hegel's approach differs from the descriptive social sciences in order to demonstrate that it can be normative. First, though, we shall have to digress into a brief discussion of Hegel's position in the philosophical tradition.

HEGEL'S SOCIAL IDEALISM AND PROGRESS

There are three characteristics of Hegel's philosophy in general of which the reader of the *Philosophy of Right* ought to be aware. One, his philosophical idealism; two, the assumption of progress implicit in his philosophy of history; and three, the difference between Hegel's absolute idealism and Kant's transcendental idealism.

Kant's transcendental idealism arose in response to the problematic assumptions of both empiricism and rationalism. Empiricism has a very simple account of knowledge: the world exerts a causal effect on the knowing faculties of the subject and the subject represents this effect to him or herself as a representation. The certainty of knowledge, then, relies on the assumption that the perceptual faculties adequately and appropriately represent the world, but there are reasons to doubt this claim: the dog sees in black and white and the human sees in colour. Is reality *in itself* colour or monochrome? One answer is to identify either the human or the dog as an ideal perceiver whose faculties deliver representations that better correspond with what is being perceived. But, we can privilege one of the faculties of knowing over the other only by making an appeal to some other story: God's providence, evolution, etc., yet none of these can be justified in the terms of empiricism itself. More sophisticated accounts of empiricism will be able to answer such objections, but the problem is that all species of empiricism must assume that perceptions adequately represent reality. And this either remains an assumption or is justified by metaphysical theories. In either case, the theory relies on a ground which is beyond the simple verification processes of empiricism. Empiricism, in short, cannot articulate a convincing account of the subject–object relation without assuming that reason is adequate and appropriate to its task.

The same problem applies to rationalism. Descartes, for example, holds that reason rather than the senses reveals the way the world actually is. However, this depends on the claim that reason is reliable, a claim Descartes himself put under question with his famous hyperbolic doubt. Of course, for Descartes this was resolved through the rational proof of the existence of a benevolent God, but the system rests on a ground that reason is unable to secure (unless one actually accepts the two arguments for the existence of God) (Descartes, 1996). Again, we have the problem with reality: in order to have knowledge, we have to assume that our reason adequately represents reality, but we cannot be certain of this given the method by which we verify our knowledge claims.

Kant overcomes this quandary by more or less ignoring the problem of reality. Intuitions are given to the mind and reason structures these so there can be an object of knowledge. Without the active participation of the thinking mind, knowledge would not be possible and so the object is *for the subject* because he or she actively constructs it. The object of knowledge is no longer to be thought of as a representation of reality because it has been worked over by the subject's reason and if knowledge is understood as correspondence with an external world, then these representations are not knowledge. But if knowledge is defined as how a rational being would perceive the object (how it would appear *for us*), then we can hang on to the notion of truth. An object, then, is empirically real if it is how a rational subject would construct the object. Truth is not true if the world is thus and so, rather it is true if rational beings would judge it to be thus and so. And since, for Kant, reason is universal – the same for all men, at all times, in all places – we will all form the same judgements if we are not partisan or irrational. The pursuit of truth is no longer the revelation of reality *in itself*, but the revelation of those categories which structure our judgements. When Hegel uses the formula I = I he is referring to the reflection of our own reason in the world when we make judgements. Interrogation of our knowledge will reveal facts about ourselves and our ways of knowing rather than facts about reality; knowledge claims are as much concerned with how we know as with what we know.

The movement from Kant to Hegel is basically about the standard of truth. Kant thinks that a subject on his own, free from corrupting influences, will be able to make true and proper judgements. Hegel disagrees: certainty can only be gained through the recognition granted by others that my judgement is correct. Truth, for Hegel, is properly interpersonal, so we replace the formula I = I with 'absolute substance which is the unity of the different independent self-consciousnesses which, in their opposition, enjoy perfect freedom and independence: "I" that is "We" and "We" that is "I"' (PhG, ¶177).[4] And the intermediate bridge is a necessary connection for knowledge claims to be true: it is no longer the case that one is correct if one reasons impartially and rationally, it also requires free and independent others to recognise your judgements as valid. Spirit, or mind [*Geist*], for Hegel is not the universal nature of the 'I think' which accompanies all the subject's representations, but an interpersonal substrate of meanings, categories and values which are shared and known to be shared (Hyppolite, 1974, 324). In other words, knowledge relies on sharing a culture with other rational beings, but if these shared meanings and categories are not constrained by the imperative to correspond to reality, then they can be different for different cultures and societies. So, how can one say that modern physics is better than mediaeval physics if all my peers agree with the latter? Can there be an external standard by which one can judge the adequacy of these meanings and categories over and above the agreement of a culture?

Let us ignore the epistemological question and concentrate on the ethical one, since it is perhaps more persuasive for us. Given the central tenets of idealism, when we state, for example, that 'all human beings are equal' or 'all men are free' we are not describing a state of affairs nor referring to some moral reality. Moral categories and concepts, axiomatic values such as equality and liberty, are categories that allow the subject to form moral judgements and are necessary for the subject to have moral experience. Though one culture may endorse liberty and equality, another may endorse order and security and their respective moral judgments will be at odds because of these axiomatic differences. And if these categories are beyond validation, then it is impossible to rationally prefer one culture to another as long as the judgement is consistent and endorsed by one's peers. Furthermore, Hegel is aware that, as abstract concepts, moral categories are too formal to dictate substantial obligations and such concrete duties can only arise from the content of a specific way of life with its implicit description of what is good (interests, welfare, respect). One may well formally state equality for all and garner much agreement, but substantially one must say what equality entails (opportunity, respect, or resources) and to whom it is to be extended (members of my class, of my nation, human beings, rational agents) and here disagreement will arise. Hegel's point is that the substantial aspect will be supplied by or be a product of my social context or moral fabric and not the workings of practical or pure reason. And this seems to open his position to the charge of relativism: we may well agree on the principle of equality or respect, but disagree for cultural reasons on how equality is to be granted and who belongs to the set of beings that merit equality.

Hence Hegel's reworking of Kant's transcendental idealism. He is aware that if the recognition of one's peers is to be an element of validation of judgements, then there is the risk that the individual who speaks the truth may well be silenced by a majority of erroneous peers or judgements may well be just expressions of cultural beliefs and beyond truth or falsehood in a robust sense. Hegel avoids such unattractive positions by appealing to history: cultural frameworks which supply one's moral obligations may become inconsistent when new moral problems cannot be adequately articulated or comprehended by the existing moral structures of experience. His most famous example is probably Sophocles' Antigone who struggles to fulfil her obligations brought about by her allegiance to her family when the laws of state conflict with these very duties (PhG, ¶470). Inconsistencies between the moral categories and the substantial content of a way of life can arise internally when people share the same structures of moral experience (Antigone) or externally when the very values which structure experience are radically different (the collision of cultures: the Aztecs and Cortés in the earlier quotation), but, according to Hegel, *progress* occurs due to these conflicts.

The task of philosophy is to become aware of this process of change and not to instigate it; to chart the re-articulation of the content and understanding of formal concepts by the process of their historical development.[5] The pure utopia ('what ideally ought to be') is unconstrained and hence an arbitrary construction of the mind. It is akin to building a house with no experience but guided only by an understanding of the laws of applied mathematics. Such a mathematician might get lucky, but he really ought to look at how buildings have been built in the past and recruit a very experienced builder if he wants to be successful. What is rational has form (the conceptual cognition of philosophy) and content (reason as substantial essence) and this content is justified through its historical development and existence:

> A further word on the subject of *issuing instructions* on how the world ought to be: philosophy, at any rate, always comes too late to perform this function. As the *thought* of the world, it appears only at a time when actuality has gone through its formative process and attained its complete state . . . When philosophy paints its grey in grey, a shape of life has grown old, and it cannot be rejuvenated, but only recognized, by the grey in grey of philosophy; the owl of Minerva begins its flight only with onset of dusk. (23)

Philosophy, it seems, has the role of explaining why we make judgements as we do rather than prescribing how we ought to make judgements.

Hegel's idea of progress is crucial to distinguish his absolute form of idealism from the transcendental idealism of Kant and to evade the charge of relativism that an individual's judgement can only be true or false with reference to a specific culture. The way to make sense of such a stance is through the enigmatic aphorism which somehow embodies the difference between transcendental idealism and absolute idealism: 'What is rational is actual;/ and what is actual is rational' (20). The aphorism has traditionally been understood in two ways: conservatively and progressively.[6] The first is consistent with the claim above that philosophy can only describe what is and not prescribe what should be; whereas the second position holds that what exists ought to be rational to be considered *actual*. Transcendental idealism holds that intuitions are the content of experience but that experience is structured by the subject. This corresponds to the second part of the aphorism, the actual has to be rational in order to be experienced. However, Hegelian absolute idealism differs in that not only does the content of experience have to have a rational structure, but the rational structure of the mind must correspond to the real structures of reality: what is rational has to be actual. So the way in which I structure experience has to conform to my peers' evaluations of the world and since Hegel seems to affirm the historical rather than the universal nature of rational categories, it seems to entail that the way in which the subject structures experience just is rational.

Hegel is most definitely not a cultural relativist nor, I would affirm, a one-dimensional conservative. The categories of understanding which structure the subject's experience must be adequate for him or her to labour in the world, and reciprocally the world has to live up to our categories – especially the moral ones. His idealism is described as absolute because one day the subject's categories of knowing will adequately fit the world and the world will have been made rational, by labour, in order to correspond to such categories, and this is guaranteed by Hegel's philosophy of history that embodies the concept of progress. This, in brief, is the end of history thesis. Human action, through the creation and refinement of social institutions and practices, moulds the world to fit the requirements of moral demands and values, whereas the interests of groups and individuals mould the rationality of these institutions to fit the demands of the world.

To use an example that is familiar to us but unknown to Hegel, moral progress in the twentieth century has been ensured through the prescription of equality, that is a demand made by reason. Such a rational demand can be made into a constitutional commitment and this changes the nature of the social world (the extension of rights to previously excluded groups, the nature of government). However, the commitment itself is modified through the pressure of civil rights movements for the extension of the principle of equality to all those who are excluded arbitrarily: women, members of other races, and so on. The nature of the actual world modifies the nature of the rational commitment. What exists, though, is part actual and part appearance. Hegel has in mind a necessary versus contingent distinction such as the swan's being a bird and its whiteness. Equality is actual, but a policy of fair opportunity is appearance, that is, it is one possible objectification (one way to interpret and substantiate its requirements) of the demand of equality. The distinction between existence and actuality opens a space for critique because as Hegel tells us: 'actuality . . . is rational through and through, and what is not rational must, for that very reason, be considered not to be actual' (EL, §142A). Both the principle of a career open to talents and the principle of equality of fair opportunity share the same rational basis, that is the theoretical demand for equality, but – perhaps – one is actual when the other is not.

THE POSSIBILITY OF IMMANENT CRITIQUE

How does Hegel avoid the charges of conservatism and relativism? The answer is that he has opened the space for an immanent as opposed to a radical critique of current social structures. The existing state of affairs, that is the contemporary and real structures of society, its practices, institutions, conventions and laws, can still fail to be actual. They may exist but not be fully rational. Social reality can fail to be actual in that it is a mere appearance and contradicts what is essential to the state. An example of this is nicely illustrated by a quotation from de Beauvoir:

According to French law, obedience is no longer included among the duties of a wife, and each woman citizen has the right to vote; but these civil liberties remain theoretical as long as they are unaccompanied by economic freedom. A woman supported by a man – wife or courtesan – is not emancipated from the male because she has a vote; if custom composes less constraint upon her than formerly, the negative freedom implied has not profoundly modified her situation; she remains bound in her condition of vassalage. It is through gainful employment that woman has traversed most of the distance that separated her from the male; and nothing else can guarantee her liberty in practice. (Beauvoir, 1997, 689)

Women may have been given the right to vote, but until the structures of the family changed and institutions and policies were introduced to give them economic freedom, then the law itself does not express the will to freedom. Progress is made possible by the demand that a law be comprehended. What is the rationality of the law to give women the vote? It is to express the principle of liberty conceived of as autonomy, yet without social structures changing, this is a hollow law since it does not achieve what it should. And this is not to be underestimated as a form of social critique. Hegel, as we shall see, does indicate where his own state has a need to make actual what is rational: a requirement of justice for trial by jury and also a need for the representation of all citizens in the political constitution. Social critique of this nature undermines the claim that Hegel's philosophy is a species of one-dimensional conservatism (the claim that it is best not to tinker with the state otherwise things may become worse), yet there is still some work to do before it can respond to the charge of relativism.

THE NEXT STEP (§4)

What, then, have we learnt from the preface and the four opening paragraphs? The philosophy of right must begin from what is given, that is those institutions, moral codes, customs and mores which constitute the realm of right, and try to sift the necessary from the contingent; that is, those conventions which are mere historical productions from those which are rational. The latter are those, one could say, that would continue to exist independent of the particular processes which brought them into being. Is the *Philosophy of Right* a piece of descriptive political science or normative political philosophy? The answer is the latter, but I hope I have shown it is so in a far more subtle way than most, more intuitive liberal accounts of critique.

The last thing we need to note is that the concept of the philosophy of right is the will (that which acts since social norms tell us what to do and what not to do), and the content of the philosophy of right is this will as actualised in the objective institutions, mores, etc., of society:

> The basis of right is the *realm of spirit* in general and its precise location and point of departure is the *will*; the will is *free*, so that freedom constitutes its substance and destiny and the system of right is the realm of actualised freedom, the world of spirit produced from within itself as a second nature. (§4)

The concept is the notion of a norm which regulates behaviour and the content of this concept is those actually existing laws, rules and conventions which regulate and coerce the behaviours of individuals. The Idea of right is the coincidence between the rational will (the will that acts freely) and rational institutions (necessary rather than merely historically contingent). The will is the translation of thought into action as a drive to give itself existence. Right is the objectified will of previous generations: it is an historically frozen normative structure which expresses the law of a rational agent given to himself. Freedom, however, is a 'destiny', a point to work towards, and we will only be truly free when the realm of right is fully rational and exists; that is, is actual. Law, for Hegel, is opposed to natural necessity. Causes tell us how human beings behave, whereas reasons tell us how they ought to behave. Contrary to social contract thinkers: the state is not an artificial structure which mediates conflicts and ensures cooperation between individuals, it is *necessary* for human freedom (FPR, §2). Central to this is the idea of a free will which legislates itself. But that cannot be taken as a given, Hegel must articulate exactly what he means by this idea and what it entails. The *Philosophy of Right* is above all a work about human freedom and we shall start by looking at our first intuitions of free will in the introduction.

Study Questions

1. Why is the faculty of understanding inappropriate for engaging in political philosophy?
2. What is the difference between a descriptive and a normative science? Is it possible to say on the basis of the content of the Preface that Hegel is engaged in a normative science?

CHAPTER 4

THE INTRODUCTION: METAPHYSICAL FREEDOM

PREAMBLE

If the *Philosophy of Right* is a normative work of political philosophy, we ought to expect it to answer some familiar questions of practical philosophy. The traditional questions of political philosophy centre on the fact that some people have the authority to regulate the behaviour of others. A man may put a gun to my head in order to direct my actions, but such a situation is surely different from the regulation of my actions by laws under threat of punishment. In the first case, we might hold that I would never choose to do as he said if it weren't for the presence of the gun, whereas in the latter case, we may argue that I would regulate my actions in accordance with the law and the dictates of the state even in the absence of the threat of punishment. Whereas the gunman has power, we might say the state has authority which is conceived as the right (and not just the capacity) to regulate my behaviour.

At the heart of the concerns of political philosophy is, then, the notion of free will. Governments and officers of the state can legitimately regulate my behaviour whereas muggers and kidnappers can only illegitimately regulate my behaviour. In both cases, Hegel controversially holds that I could have acted otherwise and the will of the state or the mugger only alters the desirability of doing one thing over another, but I am rational – according to Hegel – in acting in accordance with the dictates of state. The rules, regulations and norms of the state 'purify' my desires. The assumption that I could have acted otherwise is the assumption of the liberty of the agent that grounds normative practical philosophy. If right is to be understood as the intentions of others to make me act in a certain way, then we ought to first discuss what it is to act freely.

FREEDOM OF THE WILL (§§5–28)

If political philosophy is practical philosophy, then it concerns the will: to say that a person's actions ought to be regulated thus and so is to say that they ought to act in such and such a manner. Hegel's definition of the will is equivalent to freedom: '. . . the will is free, so that freedom constitutes its substance and destiny' (§4). We ought to notice two implicit assumptions in this quotation: one, for Hegel, a will must be free otherwise it is not a will, so freedom constitutes the will's 'substance'; and two, freedom is not a given attribute but a 'destiny' for the will to achieve. Intuitively we can understand how freedom might be an achievement: we treat adult human beings as in control of their actions, as willing their actions, but consider children, at best, only partially free. Hegel's introduction is concerned with the theoretical demonstration of these two assumptions.

Hegel identifies two accounts of freedom, both present in the philosophical tradition, which are inadequate or not properly developed:

i.   The will is free in that it is able to choose its content. Free, here, means uncaused. To be caused by a preceding event is not freedom, so whereas a man *hits* another person, a rock *collides* with a person (§5).
ii. The will is free in that it is able to satisfy its given content. Free, here, means not obstructed. A prisoner is freed when his gaol is opened (§6).

Let us discuss these in turn. Hegel's initial aim in the *Philosophy of Right* is to expose two contradictory notions of the will, both of which he finds insufficient, and present the true form on the basis of that which is partially true in each case: 'it belongs to freedom, but does not constitute the whole of freedom' (§6A). In other words, he intends to surpass each of them through a dismissal of what is false and through revealing what is true in each description. It is only this truer definition of freedom which can serve as the metaphysical basis of the description of action, ethics and politics which is to follow in his book. The reader initially finds himself faced, therefore, with two connected questions: in what way is each conception, firstly, partially true and, secondly, insufficient?

The capacity to relinquish the content of the will

We ordinarily divide the world into those things that are free and those that are not. Persons are free, most other things are not. Whereas when a rock falls on someone's head we do not – if we are not blinded by the rage of the moment – blame the object. Yet, when a man slaps my face, I do blame him because I assume that he could have done otherwise. This idea of doing otherwise is embodied in the claim that he *willed* to do what he did and was not *caused* to do as he did. What is the will? And, more significantly, when can one say a will is free as opposed to not being free? Intuitive answers include: when the will is not caused, coerced, bribed, etc. All of these are species of causes and constitute – to differing degrees – excuses for behaviour, and so a will is free when it is uncaused. Hegel thinks that such a characterisation of the will is partially correct but ultimately inadequate.

What does Hegel mean by inadequacy? Well, he means that the characterisation of the will offered is correct in some sense, but is 'Only *one aspect* of the will' (§5R) and any thinker who identifies the will wholly with it is in error since it does not exhaust the nature of the will. The first characterisation of the will emphasises this notion of a free will as an uncaused will and the capacity of the will to transcend any content:

> This will contains (α) the element of *pure indeterminacy* or of the 'I''s pure reflection into itself, in which every limitation, every content, whether present immediately through nature, through needs, desires, and drives, or given and determined in some other way, is dissolved; this is the limitless infinity of *absolute abstraction* or *universality*, the pure thinking of oneself. (§5)

The will has content in its desires or drives, but these constitute a 'limitation' and a restriction because they are *given* and not *chosen*. And one should not assume that the content of the will is only desire since, as Hegel says, the will can negate 'every limitation, every content, whether present immediately through nature, through needs, desires, and drives, or given and determined in some other way . . .'. The will can be limited in ways other than desires; its content can be given or determined by social or external conceptions. The child of a miner's family in eighteenth-century Britain would have no other choice but to become a miner, this is the truth of his predicament; the content of his will is 'generated by the concept of Spirit' (§6). However, the possibility of negating this truth, this limitation, is as real as negating one's desires. If the subject is free, he cannot be absolutely bound by his situation and the contingency of his birth. To hold a person responsible is to believe that he could have done otherwise and this is the reason we can distinguish between the husband who runs his wife down deliberately and the husband who accidentally runs down his wife because his brakes failed. The first resolves to kill his wife, wills to do it, whereas the second did not will to do so but was caused by circumstances of the situation. To be free, then, is to choose the content of one's own will and, in this way, the content of the will takes upon itself an element of self-consciousness. The subject simultaneously negates and abstracts from the desire, falling into the indeterminacy of the 'I'; the self-consciousness prior to choice that Hegel characterises as follows: 'Whatever the will has decided to choose, it can likewise relinquish' (§16). Freedom of the will is, then, the disengagement of the self, the moment when the content of the will is posited as *not me*; only by engaging with it and appropriating it can I make it *mine* again.

Hegel's claim is that the capacity to relinquish content is a necessary element in an account of human freedom since we do describe coerced and hypnotised agents as not free. And the reason is that they are unable to relinquish the content of their will which has been imposed on them from the outside. Yet, Hegel's hesitation over the first conception of the will is that if one identifies it as the complete characterisation of human freedom, the error leads to danger. The disengagement of the self from all content, a self which is reflected into itself and dissolves into empty universality: 'the pure thinking of oneself' becomes the paradigm of human freedom and the will is conceived as that which thinks, that which exists prior to and independent from its thoughts. One is free when one's thoughts are produced uncaused and not free when thoughts are determined by preceding events. For any representation there must exist a subject who has that representation and is not identical with that representation; the infinite, universal 'I'. In other words, it is the realm of self-consciousness without content, which takes itself as content and apprehends nothing, for a self-consciousness without an object is empty. For Hegel, this conception of the will has undesirable practical consequences when it is made actual (that is, acted upon) because 'whatever such freedom believes that it wills can in itself be no more than abstract representation, and its actualization can only be the fury of destruction' (§5R). Hegel sees two practical problems with the identification of the will with the capacity to relinquish its content: it is, firstly, *ineffectual* and, secondly, *dangerous*.

The free will understood in this way is a 'flight from every content as a limitation' (§5R). Such a flight is best exemplified by the religious attitudes of the Hindu Brahmin and the holding oneself out into the nothingness of being. It is also a theoretical position which, due to its ascetic repulsion of all practical contents of the will, offers little chance of constructing an ethics with which to live one's life. Hegel sees these as symptomatic of the realm of the Understanding which abstracts and reasons but is unable to act. However, the purely formal will is contradictory because even thinking is activity for Hegel, and activity produces objects. The 'I' translates its subjectivity into objectivity through will and a will that does not act is no will at all. Actions, even thinking, are the expression of the will in the world and to seek to annihilate oneself, as the Brahmin does, is to be involved in a contradictory enterprise that is impossible (§§8–9).

More worryingly, such an attitude is dangerous. Such negative universality, if it does seek to act upon the world, to assert its own existence, is necessarily destructive because it has to reject what is given for the sake of rejecting it. For Hegel, this negative universality expressed itself historically in the Terror following the French Revolution:

> If it remains theoretical, it becomes in the religious realm the Hindu fanaticism of pure contemplation; but if it turns to actuality, it becomes in the realm of both politics and religion the fanaticism of destruction, demolishing the whole existing social order, eliminating all individuals regarded as suspect by a given order, and annihilating any organisation which attempts to rise up anew. Only in destroying something does this negative will have a feeling of its own existence. (§5R)

If I am free when I am not caused, then to be free I have to refuse and reject every possible cause and that means – from moment to moment – destroying what is before me. The heroes of existentialist and nihilist literature are characterised by the will to refuse the norms and conventions of the social world because they feel unfree before them.[1] Every motivation which arises for a reason is an instance of inauthenticity, yet Hegel would stress that this retreat into the 'I' can offer no authentic attitudes at all. The reason to resist determining structures is simply because they are determining, not because of anything about their content. The attitude relies on the concepts and demands of abstract understanding and it is expressed in the desire to make the world meet the requirements of formal reason:

> An example of this was the Terror in the French Revolution, during which all differences of talents and authority were supposed to be cancelled out. This was a time of trembling and quaking and of intolerance towards everything particular. For fanaticism wills only what is abstract, not what is articulated, so that whenever differences emerge, it finds them incompatible with its own indeterminacy and cancels them. This is why the people, during the French Revolution, destroyed once more the institutions they had themselves created, because all institutions are incompatible with the abstract self-consciousness of equality. (§5A)

The demand for equality, made by reason on a world not ready for it, motivated the refusal of leaders after leaders since equality demanded pure equality. It is the centrifugal force of the *no*, the way it is easy to refuse, to negate, to show one's power over the world by negating and destroying it. Hegel predicts that the actualisation of negativity is necessarily destructive. One destroys the good with the bad: even if I knew it were right to x, this knowledge itself becomes the reason not to x. When applied to the practical project of right the realm of impersonal universality is a foundation built in sand. Absolute negativity, the freedom to negate every content of the will, is a logical possibility, but for Hegel, the Terror and Hinduism are pathological or symptomatic of the will's logical freedom.

After such damning comments, it would be worthwhile to remind ourselves of the partial truth of this form of the will: it can 'relinquish' content, that is the will is the possibility to do otherwise than one did. Politically, this ability to relinquish content and, therefore, be responsible for what one does plays a pivotal role in moral freedom and also in the demand that the content of the will be subjectively endorsed which, for Hegel, is the basis of the subjective will of the Enlightenment and its refusal of blind obedience to authority.

Empirical freedom

The second characterisation of the will concerns the particularity and finitude of the will:

> (β) In the same way, 'I' is the transition from undifferentiated indeterminacy to *differentiation, determination*, and the *positing* of a determinacy as a content and object. – This content may further be given by nature, or generated by the concept of spirit. Through this positing of itself as something *determinate*, 'I' steps into existence in general – the absolute moment of the *finitude* or *particularisation* of the 'I'. (§6)

The will can be equated with the conscious act of pursuing a desire; when I desire an object, the will is that which desires. It is free if it can satisfy this desire and not free if it is obstructed from satisfaction. In the simplest case, if you tie me to the chair, you obstruct me from satisfying my desire to go to the cinema; if you put me in gaol, you constrain and limit my possible satisfaction of a whole range of objects. Hegel holds that the particularisation of the will – its limitation through its content – is an instance of freedom, or rather freedom *in itself*. The will is simply the process of willing an object of desire and an agent is merely the representation of this act of willing. Freedom of the will is, on this account, an external matter: it is freedom from constraint, the capacity to satisfy desire without obstruction from external forces.

The capacity for satisfaction is, of course, an essential part of Hegel's conception of freedom. It is for this reason that he refers to this as freedom *in itself* (and spontaneity as freedom *for itself*), which is to say only that such a description implicitly discloses freedom, albeit in its simplest and most immediate form. Drives and desires immediately encountered in the will constitute its finitude, its limitation. Why is the empirical characterisation of freedom in itself and the metaphysical, spontaneous account of free will for itself? Hegel tells us: 'The will which is free as yet only in itself is the immediate or natural will.' In other words, the will encounters its own freedom in rational desire whose rationality – due to its immediacy – is hidden or 'does not yet have the form of rationality'. The subject apprehends this will as its own, but in this abstraction posits a difference between its content and the subject's form: 'but this form and that content are still different, so that the will is a finite will within itself' (§11). The will is finite because its content is given and its form predetermined and thus the subject is not aware of it as his own. Desire allows man to act rationally on the world in attaining his ends. An end is given which – through action – man realises, that is makes actual, in the world. It reveals the necessity of this aspect of the will for Hegel, that is its limitation as solely freedom in itself, not yet a freedom aware of itself and therefore not full human freedom. The reasons for action on which the agent acts are, as yet, only rational in themselves and not for the agent. Hegel dismisses this as an adequate account of human subjectivity. For him, the model of desire as a theory of action cannot fully explain human behaviour even if it reveals the necessity of this aspect of the will.

Such an account cannot be a full description of the freedom of the will since it rests on two presuppositions: first, that human action is to be based on a desiring model of cause and effect; and secondly, reason cannot motivate action since it arises in response to a desire and not as the cause of a desire. This would of course relegate reason to a secondary role as either – at worst – inert, passive and reflective; or – more sensibly – as that which implements the course of action to which desire is aimed, giving rise to the famous Humean position: 'Reason is, and ought only to be, the slave of the passions, and can never pretend to any other office than to serve and obey them' (Hume, 1962, 127). Hegel views this account of the will as radically incomplete: if the idea of the desiring subject were to be an adequate account of subjectivity, then it has to explain how the agent resolves *which* desires to satisfy and *in what particular way* to satisfy them. At any one time there are a multitude of desires present to the subject with myriad possible objects of satisfaction, 'The system of this content as it is already present in its immediacy in the will exists only as a multitude of varied drives, each of which is mine in general along with others. . .' and these desires are general in nature (thirst, sex, hunger, etc.), '. . . something universal and intermediate which has all kinds of objects and can be satisfied in all kinds of ways'

(§12). So, without recourse to a selection process, how can this account of the will offer an explanation of how, where and when the desire is to be satisfied since desires themselves cannot explain which and how alone. Hegel's claim is that no theory of this form can avoid explaining resolution without recourse to the concept of a will that chooses: 'Inasmuch as the will, in this double indeterminacy, gives itself the form of individuality, it is a resolving will, and only in so far as it makes any resolutions at all is it an actual will' (§12).

There is a clue to how Hegel's own distinction between in itself and for itself can be mapped on to and used to criticise any claim that the notion of the free will is exhausted by the idea of external freedom:

> The animal, too, has drives, desires, and inclinations, but it has no will and must obey its drive if nothing external prevents it. But the human being, as wholly indeterminate, stands above his drives and can determine and posit them as his own. The drive is part of nature, but to posit it in this 'I' depends upon my will, which therefore cannot appeal to the fact that the drive is grounded in nature. (§11A)

Hegel, here, has in his sights any claim that human behaviour can be reduced to a naturalistic story about primary drives, their collisions and resolution. The natural will is free in itself, because it expresses the relationship of the will to the world, yet the will is not yet the human's own. It has been given to him or her. It becomes for itself when the human being has reflected upon it and either endorsed or substituted it for another drive; then the will is free for itself, but this relies on the capacity to relinquish its content, a capacity which is peculiarly human. Any reductivist account of the will cannot explain the will but merely negate it: there is no such thing as a resolving will, only the expression of a deep collision of drives. A naturalist such as Hobbes might tell us that talk of a liberty of will is a mistake of language, much the same as to talk of a liberty of speech. Speech doesn't have liberty, but the agent who wishes to speak has liberty to do so. Similarly, the will doesn't have liberty (a mistake of language), but the agent who wishes to act has liberty to do so and that is all the will amounts to (Hobbes, 1982, Chap. 21). The will is nothing but the strongest desire, that is the desire acted upon. Hence, we are in the realm of simple causality.

Why is the reductivist's account of freedom inadequate? The 'I' which resolves is the 'I' that identifies a desire as 'mine' and resolves to satisfy it. When a one-year-old boy chooses a CD from the stack before him, it tells us nothing about him. His action is random and arbitrary; he is 'acting without a guiding principle' (§294R). True human action is different: the objects of our desires are the expressions of a resolution on the part of an 'I' who is then identified by his or her choices: 'By resolving, the will posits itself as the will of a specific individual and as a will which distinguishes itself from everything else' (§13). Imagine that I desire to buy a new car. I go to the forecourt and desire a particular car – but can the salesman swipe that away and substitute it by any other car? No, the object is not substitutable even if the desire is the same: the desire to own a car. I want a particular car and not just a car. The 'I' identifies a moment of resolution, of decision on an agent's part. Any reductivist account of human behaviour seeks to reduce the moment of decision to nothing but the expression of desires, the strongest is the one which appears to win out in an illusory deliberation. However, such a theory is unable to explain anything because if a good becomes that which is desired and it cannot be other than this otherwise reason would be able to prioritise desires, then desires cannot be good or bad in themselves. There can be – on this account – no way to rank desires, exclude them or to compare them. There exists no 'yardstick' and our action is not free but is merely a given impulse (§§17–18).

Hegel would claim in response that one cannot negate the will since there is always a 'resolving will': the 'I' chooses this particular object and the particular way in which to satisfy his or her desire. No general account of drives can adequately explain how the one desire amongst many is selected nor how that desire takes on its particular expression. To say the strongest desire is the one which is expressed is empty as it amounts to saying that the one which has been expressed is the one which has been expressed. The will had to be the moment of resolution and, if the resolution is not an expression of rational choice, it is once more arbitrary and not free. Hegel's criticisms against the naturalists' hope of reducing human behaviour to a set of common drives and the relationships between them sometimes sounds as though he begs the question. The reductivist programme may just be interested in redefining or excluding the notion of a will from descriptions of human behaviour and since the will is the starting point of Hegel's political philosophy, he is unable to truly embrace such a movement. However, it is when we look at the transition from Abstract Right to Morality due to the requirement of the concept of responsibility in the description of human action, that many of his points become more salient. Abstract right is, after all, the development of a system of right based on the idea of empirical freedom and it is woefully inadequate. For Hegel, to reduce the human being to an animal undermines notions of responsibility and freedom and the reductivist is then forced into very unconvincing explanations of certain behaviour patterns of human beings.[2]

In what way, though, is such an account partially true? The separation of subject (I) from object (need) is an embryonic form of freedom since satisfaction is gained through unity. It is this truth of the will which forms a basis for ethical and rational action: 'Thus enjoyment in which the object is determined purely ideally, and entirely annihilated, is purely sensuous enjoyment; i.e., the satiation which is the restoration of the indifference and emptiness of the individual or of his bare possibility of being ethical or rational' (SS, 105). It is the 'possibility' because it demonstrates the subject's power over desire and the world through acting on reasons; but it is 'bare' because the content of the will has not been freely, that is rationally, chosen.

Self-determination

Having dismissed the two most common accounts of free will, Hegel proceeds to offer an account of freedom as self-determination, embodying the insights of both these conceptions, but resisting the tendency to exhaust the meaning of human freedom by exclusively aligning it with their own descriptions:

(γ) The will is the unity of both these moments – *particularity* reflected *into itself* and thereby restored to *universality*. It is *individuality*, the *self-determination* of the 'I', in that it posits itself as the negative of itself, that is, as *determinate* and *limited*, and at the same time remains with itself, that is, in its *identity with itself* and universality; and in this determination, it joins together with itself alone. – 'I' determines itself in so far as it is the self-reference of negativity. As this *reference to itself*, it is likewise indifferent to this determinacy; it knows the latter as its own and as *ideal*, as a mere *possibility* by which it is not restricted but in which it finds itself merely because it posits itself in it. (§7)

The first conception of freedom accurately describe the will's capacity to relinquish its contents, but, if it is the be all and end all of freedom, it proposes a will which is without necessity and arbitrary: it becomes either the absence of action and willing (Brahmin) or the mere whim of asserting whatever is its content at that time (Absolute Terror). The second conception of the will correctly describes the particularity of the 'I' as opposed to the universal, but if it is the whole extent of the will it is mere external necessity and, again, nothing but a will which allows desires and drives to be expressed without reflection and hence arbitrarily. Hegel talks of inner necessity, when the subject chooses the content of his will in relation to external and rational reasons, and this is the apex of freedom:

> A freedom that had no necessity within it, and a mere necessity without freedom, are determinations that are abstract and hence untrue. Freedom is essentially concrete, eternally determinate within itself, and thus necessary at the same time. When people speak of necessity, it is usually initially understood as just determination from without; for instance, in finite mechanics, a body moves only when another body collides with it, and precisely in the direction imparted to it by this collision. This is merely external necessity, however, not a genuinely inner necessity, for that is freedom. (EL, §35A)

Freedom is, then, self-determination which is neither without 'necessity' (spontaneity) or with necessity but without 'freedom' (empirical freedom) and is characterised as independence: 'Only in this freedom is the will completely *with itself* (*bei sich*) because it has reference to nothing but itself, so every relationship of *dependence* on something *other* than itself is thereby eliminated' (§23).[3] Full human freedom can only be free in-itself-for-itself: 'Only when the will has itself as its object is it *for-itself* what it is *in-itself* (§10). The question, then, must be: what is it for the will to act freely (in itself) and to take acting freely as its object (for itself)?

The best way to make sense of this new conception of freedom and the implicit Hegelian language is to discuss a rather distasteful example. Imagine walking home one night to hear the rather feeble, but anguished, cries of a cat. You see before you a cat that has been hit by a car with its belly open and its pitiful eyes turned towards you, imploringly. It is obvious that the cat has no chance, would not be saved by a veterinary surgeon even if you could take it there on time and, most important of all, the cat is in insufferable agony. It seems there is but one pressing choice facing you: should you kill the cat to ease its suffering or should you flee from the scene without doing a thing.

If we consider freedom in-itself, that is the acting on external necessity without being obstructed from fulfilling our desire, then one's immediate inclination might be to flee the horror of the scene, close all our windows to block out the anguished cries and sleep the dilemma off, since in the morning all will be much better. In this case, one is free to the extent you are able to flee and escape the cries, that is to the extent you can satisfy your desire (that is, repress and hide from the starkness of the cat's suffering). However, such a choice cannot be described as 'free' since it depends wholly on the moral luck of one's character: the first passer-by may be forthright and resolute and able to kill the cat whereas the second might be cowardly and sensitive and unable to carry out the act. So, it is arbitrary what happens depending on what character one naturally possesses and this is not a matter of free choice.

And if we consider freedom for-itself, that is, the capacity to relinquish the content of one's will, then we might want to retreat into the infinity of the 'I' and content ourselves with the thought that our choices do not matter. We might say that it neither matters *to us* whether the cat dies or lives and each choice is equally valid: to choose to do nothing, to kill the cat or to flee. To choose to do nothing is, however, to choose to let the cat die. To choose to kill the cat is a mere expression, once more, of preference and is arbitrary, not a matter of a free choice since no choosing takes place, only a spontaneous occurrence: 'consciousness is filled in such a way that its content is not derived from its own self-determining activity as such' (§15R).

Hegel's real contention with the two conceptions of freedom commonly held in the philosophical tradition is that they cannot account for full human freedom, that they are an inaccurate description of the human condition. And one can see in this case that he perhaps has a point. On being confronted with such a scene, the human being would normally be assailed by myriad reactions:

sympathy, horror, compassion, revulsion, duty, indifference, curiosity, fear, a sense of righteousness, etc., all of which propose a different course of action. This plurality of possible motivations is what Hegel refers to as the 'system of all drives' and the identity of the subject is with each and every one of these drives, not just one as the second conception of freedom holds nor with something independent and indifferent to them as the first conception of freedom holds (§17R). Yet, these reactions are firstly encountered as 'other', as imposing themselves on us from outside. The free will is, for Hegel, the transition from the system of all drives to the 'rational system of the will's determination' via the *'purification of the drives'* (§19).

Let us extend our example: I am repulsed by the scene, the blood and gore and the pitiful cries of a dying animal. My immediate reaction is to flee, to run away and I perhaps placate myself with the simple excuse that I could do nothing, that it was not up to me to do anything. But, simultaneously, I feel the weight of the burden of a duty: to free the animal from suffering. All I have to do is bring a rock down on the cat's head and I will have done it a service, done what I know *should be done*. Of the two people described earlier, I want to be the resolute and brave man and not the sensitive coward, but I do not want to be insensible, nor callous (laughing as I bring down the rock). I want to act as I believe a good person would act. So, of the two desires 'I want to flee' and 'I want to kill the cat' it is the latter I prioritise: I want to be the sort of person who can kill the cat, that is 'I want to want to kill the cat'. The desire to modify oneself is simply the desire to have certain desires and needs as one's own so that they no longer confront me as 'other'.[4] Contemporary philosophical language will help us here: a first-order desire is the simple formula 'I want to x' whereas the second-order desire is the endorsement of this desire as valid: 'I want to want to x' (Frankfurt, 1982; Taylor, 1977, 1982). Such endorsement involves the transcendence implicit in the first conception of freedom, the relinquishment of the immediate content of the will, and also the determination of the second since to 'want to want' is a consideration of the whole system of drives and the will's assertion of the value of one above others which is not merely arbitrary.

However, we must qualitatively distinguish between two types of choices. The first type is insignificant, as say the choice between having broccoli or carrots as a side vegetable for my tea tonight.

Such a choice can only be arbitrary since there would not normally be any necessary reason for choosing one over the other, and in cases such as these the human being scans and traverses his or her desires without evaluation, as I would the contents of my sock drawer. For Hegel, indifferent choices such as these hardly matter to one's overall way of life; they are not truly second-order desires (Wood, 1990, part 1, chap. 3). It is the second type of choice which is perhaps more interesting: the desire is evaluated and articulated in terms of values. Crucial choices matter because they alter the person who we are. As a human, one is capable of evaluating one's desires – choosing between them – but also evaluating one's being, trying to create a certain person with specific desires and without certain others; that is, to determine oneself.

I become *me* by selecting certain desires. These desires fill the will and manifest themselves through action on the world, the effect of which is their embodiment in the world and the projection of myself onto the world. They are constitutive of my identity. The second-order desires involved in deep evaluation are those that determine us as individuals. The second type of evaluation is perhaps best exemplified by returning to the example of the dying cat. The choice is stark: kill the cat and relieve its suffering, or leave it alone and run away. It would not be contentious, I think, to assume most people are guilty of bad faith in such a situation, that most would recognise that the *right* action would be to kill it, yet most would flee. The point of the example is that one should choose to resist one's immediate desire and act on motivations one sees not as other but as – in some sense – one's own. To act on motivations which are worthwhile or, simply put, values. I want to want to end the cat's suffering because it is *good*. To be a good human, I should kill the cat. It is at this point that freedom invokes the notion of morality and ethics because it is clear that at issue here are those values which one would term ethical: compassion, benevolence, *et al.* The desire to kill that cat, if it can be called such, reflects a higher motive on the part of the human and a better personality. The point of this example is that children (and a few adults) would be unable to articulate the matter in hand so as to help them overcome the immediacy of their desire – and its simultaneous emotional expression: horror, curiosity – because they are not fully developed people. One's character can be perfected by society and by development through education; it is not fixed by one's birth or by one's nature.

Certain desires possess qualities which can be articulated and, as they can be articulated, they can be objectified. For example, in the cat case, there is the compassion of extinguishing the cat's suffering which explains and justifies what is normally an abhorrent act. This is a *crucial* decision; it is one that determines who one is. Whether I eat a Mars bar or a scotch egg does, in a limited sense, determine a 'me' in the world; it is not, though, crucial to the essence I wish to create for myself. My decision in the cat situation will, however, have *worth* and *value*. Of course, this does depend on a particular person, but it is easy to see that two levels of being are here called into question; two different kinds of choices: 'deep' – those concerned with who one is and how others perceive one – and 'shallow' or everyday choices. Articulation is the method through which reason is made manifest, and reason manifests itself through the postulation of values. What, then, are values? We can perhaps say that values are motivations or desires *worth having* (Wolf, 1990, 49). The human desires to be motivated by certain values, be they benevolence or charity, and in so doing expresses these values or reasons for action as universally good things to possess. Furthermore, when asked why one acted so, the response will be articulate and persuasive; it will not be a shrug of the shoulders and a grunt. As these articulations can be objectified, they become values which are seen as indispensable for the good human to possess. And their justification to a large extent depends on their possible articulation and endorsement by other agents and, as such, they become objective in the sense of being independent of a particular subject.

The will is an expression of reason as instantiated in the qualitative difference between shallow and deep choices: certain choices are easy because there exists a reason to act one way rather than another. If the cat were not so badly hurt and I evaluated my desire to flee as an expression of my horror, I would quickly reject it and take the cat to a veterinary surgeon. If I did not and I claimed to be a compassionate person then people would disagree. (Please note that this is still a deep choice, even if it is an easily resolvable one.) Compassion is a motivation worth having, whereas revulsion (in this case) is not. Thus, the purification of drives will be the operation of reason on one's storehouse of drives and desires in order to make me want to be compassionate. These values are, then, objective goods because they trump the mere subjective will.

The purification of drives, though, reveals a schism between what I immediately want and what I ought to want which may, by chance, coincide, but most often will not. This division at the heart of the self reveals more clearly than anything else Hegel's debt to a tradition of freedom that is, at best, alien and, at worst, suspicious to Anglo-Saxon philosophy. We in the Anglophone world are very much influenced by the empirical, scientific account of the will, first given a philosophically sophisticated account in Hobbes: freedom is the freedom to satisfy one's desires (Hobbes, 1982, chap. 21). This is, of course, Hegel's second conception of freedom and we need not recapitulate his rejection of it. But there exists a very different tradition, finding its origin in Rousseau, concerning the discussion of freedom (Rousseau, 1997, books 1 and 2).[5]

Rousseau believed that society corrupted man, that the conventions, laws and prescriptions of culture – what Hegel calls *Sittlichkeit* or ethical life – determine what is right and wrong and the man feels compelled to obey such motivations. Thus, the self is divided between what it wants and what it thinks is right, yet for the most part what it wants does not coincide with what it thinks is right since the values of society are in the interests of a specific class and not the individual man. Rousseau celebrates the noble savage because he is not bound by external laws and values and is able to act on his pure desires, those of egoism tempered by compassion. These desires trump others and the noble savage obeys his own conscience. He was free to do as he wished and what he wished was right. However, society has moulded man so that what he wants – what he desires – has also been corrupted. Rousseau believes man cannot return to the purity of the noble savage due to the corruption of society, but can gain an equal if different type of freedom. Man will be free only when what he wants is what is right, so that he willingly acts so as to attain the good. In our example of the dying cat: my desires must be moulded so that I am the sort of person who wants what is right, that is, the cat's release from suffering. Of course, in contemporary society: what is right and wrong needs to be rationalised since the current laws are not the expression of freedom and equality so dear to Rousseau and also men need to be changed – through the coercion and influence of specific institutions – so that they want the right things. Rousseau sees freedom as the union of the moral and desiring selves in one person: I am free when I act on laws which I myself have endorsed (when what is right and wrong is an expression of myself and thus desired by myself). The two selves then are: the particular self (what I want) and the social/moral self (what I think is right) and freedom consists in the union of these two. This is achieved for Rousseau when I determine what is right and wrong, that is legislate the laws and values of society, and also act upon them; in other words, I legislate myself. So, freedom is an activity which either changes what I want (through social pressure, coercion, desirability) or changes what I believe to be right/rational (through the objective determinations of good, that is through my values taken to be valid). The determination of what is right and wrong, though, is not purely an act of individual reason (as Kant supposed), but is a social activity: what is accepted by all within my community as right is what is right (the general will). Freedom is thus communal social activity. Freedom, then, is not the possibility of acting but a special type of action: self-legislation, that is actions which are entirely determined by myself and not at all by external influences or factors.

Self-determination for Hegel is the process whereby man actualises his true essence, that is freedom. In-itself man is freedom, that is the essence of the will. Therefore, the will must become for-itself freedom, that is it must express its freedom to the world through its acts. It cannot do this with the aid of the arbitrary will since this is not human freedom, it is only freedom in-itself. To be free for-itself, the will must instead project an image of man as he *should* be and make those values *his* own. And these values will only become mine when they are not Other, that is I comprehend and recognise them as good.

Man's actualisation of that which he is in-itself requires constant labour and making those things which are initially opposed to one's being, part of one's being and overcoming them. And this is what separates Hegel from Rousseau. He differs from Rousseau because he does not believe the noble savage to be an example of freedom and such a difference undermines, for Hegel, the whole social contract approach to political justification. Freedom is properly understood as the unity of the particular self and the social, ethical self but this is only possible when the subject is 'at home' or 'with himself', or when the will 'remains with itself' or has '*identity with itself*': ' "I" is at home in the world when it knows it, and even more so when it has comprehended it' (§4A). Again, we have the appeal to comprehension, that is, to be able to grasp the inner rationality of a drive or a motivation. For Rousseau, the noble savage is at home with himself because what he wants is what is right because it is natural and uncorrupted, but for Hegel, there is no objectivity and the noble savage is nothing but an animal: acting on immediate desires that are external to him. It is only 'As spirit, man is a free being who is in a position not to let himself be determined by natural drives. When he exists in an immediate and uncivilized condition, he is therefore in a situation in which he ought not to be, and from which he must liberate himself' (§18A). Man must replace his natural existence with a rational, social existence (spirit). The free will acts from inner necessity when what the subject wants is the right or rational thing to do. But this, of course, depends upon knowing what is the right thing to do and Hegel sees this as derivable from the moral fabric of one's community, the conventions, laws, values and virtues one shares with others and can justify to others.

Society is, then, necessary for full human freedom because only in that society where the values are objectively true can the human being comprehend the obligations and drives which confront him as his own rather than other. And this is the destiny of spirit because:

> man *has* by nature a drive towards right, *and also* a drive towards property and morality, *and also* a drive towards sexual love, a drive towards sociability, etc. . . . man finds within himself, as a *fact of his consciousness*, that he wills right, property, the state, etc. This same content, which appears here in the shape of drives, will recur later in another form, namely that of *duties*. (§19R)

Rational drives actualise themselves in society as rights, duties and values, that is objectively – held by all men – desirable motivations. The human wills social institutions because these are necessary for freedom and not as the social contract tradition holds because they are a necessary compromise and limitation on freedom. Without society, culture and a shared moral fabric, man cannot be free and hence cannot be man because there can be no necessity to his actions. Yet, one's social fabric may just become a second nature and be as determinate as one's natural will. The human being is only free when the dictates and regulations of his society are comprehended, and in comprehension the subject feels at home because he wills that which he thinks is right. Dictates and laws are no longer external, but are freely self-imposed because the subject could always act otherwise, but does not since he sees the law or institution as right. So to be free I must want to kill the cat and know that this is the right thing to do. The social and moral fabric which exists outside of me, but within which I feel at home, supplies the certainty of rightness for the act. Of course, the standard of rightness cannot be a mere feeling of homeliness, since most persons would feel at home in their own culture and with what is familiar and may well be in error. How do we know that our society, with its laws and institutions, is rational? The answer to that question constitutes the rest of the book, but the introduction concludes with a consideration of the theoretical framework in which to understand Hegel's reply to this question.

ACTUALISATION AND HEGEL'S CONCEPTION OF INTERNAL NECESSITY

Self-determination is a process of actualisation and not a given attribute of human beings; we are not born as self-legislators but must become so. Hegel holds that the goal of history is for man to rationalise himself. Man is potentially rational, but not actually rational. Man begins his life with immediate desires and meanings which govern his action. The meaning of his action is given. However, through reflection and transcendence man is able to articulate the deep reasons for his action. He works himself over and rationalises his behaviour through articulating the true reasons for action: 'When reflection applies itself to the diverse drives, representing them, estimating them, and comparing them with one another . . . it confers *formal universality* upon this material and purifies it, in this external manner, of its crudity and barbarity' (§20). Actualisation resides in making man's potential and latent rationality govern his desires.

The whole of the process of actualisation is described by Hegel in an early work in a very succinct, but precise, manner:

> The world does not come to this [new] consciousness as a process as it did previously in the abstract form of *something external*, for it has been presented thoroughly by the form of consciousness; [the child's] inorganic nature is the *knowledge of his parents*, the world is already prepared [on his behalf]; and it is the form of *ideality* which comes to the child. Since the world comes to the evolving consciousness as this ideal world, the problem for consciousness is

to find meaning, the reality of this ideal, to find out how the ideal exists; it must realise this ideality. (JR1, 234)

First, the world is not presented initially to consciousness in the being of knowledge, rather the world is a construction of reasons for action. Such reasons at the deepest level are probably based on the biology of a creature: it is just that it is the way that it is that it acts like that. Reasons for action are also embodied in social customs and they do not only come from what we are, but also from what we have made of ourselves. Humans not only have immediate biological reasons for action, but also sociological reasons for action. I shall expand this theme as the book continues, but will only touch on the subject here in a preliminary manner. How we act, the reasons for action we possess, derive in a large part from our form of life: 'The cultivation of the universality of thought is the absolute value of *education*' (§20, see also §151). By *form of life* I mean that which Hegel calls *Sittlichkeit* or those values and norms which govern the subject's practical reasoning deriving from his role in, and being a member of, a certain society.

In the above quotation, Hegel uses the term 'ideality' to refer to the child's form of life or moral-value map of the world. Social meanings are objectified in the world and the child 'sees as', that is in terms of these values. The child possesses the reason, meanings and values of his tradition *in itself*. They are ready at hand to use and constitute the child's pre-understanding. However, as such, the child is not free, he is no better than the animal acting in accordance with reasons only because that is just the way he is:

> Freedom is only present where there is no other for me that is not myself. The natural man, who is determined only by his drives, is not at home with himself; however self-willed he may be, the *content* of his willing and opining is not his own, and his freedom is only a *formal* one. (EL, §23, second addition)

Like the natural man, the Hobbesian model of social man is not free because he is not *at home* with himself. To be at home with himself, the content of his will must be *his own* and there must be 'no other for me that is not myself'. These others are the dictates of society, the conditions of one's way of life, that demand that I conform with them. Only when I am at home in these regulations am I truly free.

How is this rationalisation possible? When Hegel proposes that '. . . self-consciousness is *Desire* in general', he places himself in direct confrontation with Kant (PhG, ¶167). Whereas the latter wanted to ostracise all phenomenal aspects – including desire – from the noumenal, understanding self, Hegel sees that desire has to be a condition for the possibility of experience: the world exists *for me*. Without desire, man would not have reasons for action and would not, consequently, have knowledge. The world, in its immediate form, confronts consciousness as a system of reasons for action and their relevant desires. Only through acting, only through reflection on these primary reasons for action, can man articulate new ones and compare them with other goods. The possibility of articulation of reasons for action is based on the fundamental mode of being a desiring subject. Similarly, it relies on the ability to transcend the immediate situation and its claims. The fundamental desire of self-consciousness is to make reasons for action for itself; that is, to actualise the rationality of its actions. Self-consciousness desires to be rational, that is just the kind of thing man is.

The 'problem for consciousness' is, as Hegel says, to realise – that is, *actualise* – this social ideality and to rationally legitimise the social determinations of one's form of life into internal necessity. The subject is at home with himself when he acts from reasons in themselves rational (that is, they can be articulated and accepted by his form of life) and for themselves rational (the agent recognises the goal of the action as a good):

> The ethical person is conscious of the content of his action as something necessary, something that is valid in and for itself; and this consciousness is so far from diminishing freedom, that, on the contrary, it is only through this consciousness that his abstract freedom becomes a freedom that is actual and rich in content, as distinct from freedom of choice [*Willkür*], a freedom that still lacks content and is merely possible. (EL, §158A)

SUBJECTIVE AND OBJECTIVE WILL (§§25–26)

Freedom for-itself, spontaneity, can only offer a will which is totally subjective and not free because it is meaningless and arbitrary. Freedom in-itself, empirical freedom, can only offer a will which is totally objective and not free because it acts under external and not internal necessity. In articulating our desires, in evaluating them and denoting them either right or wrong, freedom is actualised as reason; when one's free choices coincide with rational choice, one has mastered one's nature and is fully free. Hegel holds the Rousseauian aspiration for freedom as unity: when what I subjectively desire is what is objectively right.[6]

Hegel warns his audience against the purely subjective will:

> The *subjective*, as far as the will in general is concerned, denotes the will's self-conscious aspect, its individuality as *distinct from* its concept which has being *in itself*. The subjectivity of the will therefore denotes (α) *pure form*, the *absolute unity* of the self-consciousness with itself, in which the self-consciousness, as 'I' = 'I', is totally inward and *abstractly* dependent on itself – i.e. the pure *certainty* of itself, as distinct from truth; (β) the *particularity* of the will as arbitrariness and as the contingent content of whatever ends the will may pursue; (γ) one-sided form in general, in so far as that which is willed, whatever its content, is still only a content belonging to the self-consciousness, an unaccomplished end. (§25)

A will is subjective in three ways: (a) as being that which is chosen by the self and not external causes; (b) as being identifiable with an individual who wills; and (c) not yet objectified through action. But a subjective will is not free if, to return to our earlier example, I kill the cat because of immediate inclination or do so arbitrarily, without good reason. In both cases I want to kill the cat, but in neither case can the motivation be described as properly my own, according to Hegel. The subjective will is only free if it can externalise its reason for action in terms that are acceptable as right to one's social community.

Secondly, Hegel warns us against the totally objective will:

> (α) The will, in so far as it has itself as its determination and is thus in conformity with its concept and truly itself, is the *totally objective will*; (β) but the *objective* will, inasmuch as it *lacks the infinite form* of self-consciousness, is the will immersed in its object or condition, whatever the content of the latter may be – it is the will of the child, the ethical will, or the will of the slave, the superstitious will, etc.; (γ) finally, *objectivity* is the one-sided form

opposed to the subjective determination of the will and is thus the immediacy of existence as *external* existence; the will does not become *objective* to itself in this sense until its ends are fulfilled. (§26)

A will is objective if it (a) acts on a self-imposed law and does what is right; (b) acts purely on authority, through a trust of the law (child) or coercion (slave) imposed on it and does not subjectively see the law as a good only the obedience to the legislator as a good; and (c) a will is objectified in the action on the world: my desire to eat the cake becomes objective in the consumption of the cake (my intention can be adequately reconstructed by an other agent who observes my action).[7] (c) can be ignored here, it comes into play later.[8] A totally objective will may do what is right, but does not do so freely. So, if we return once more to the cat example, my will is superstitious if I kill the cat because I am instructed to by the authoritative voice of the priest (I fear going to Hell); or my will is that of the slave if I kill the cat because an animal lover puts a gun to my head; or my will is ethical (in a pejorative sense that Hegel does not use consistently) or that of a child if I kill the cat because it is the done thing.

Hegel wants freedom to be the union of the subjective and the objective wills. The subjective is necessary for the will to be at home in the regulations of society, and the regulations of society are necessary for the will not to be arbitrary. So, for example, the right thing to do is to wear the seatbelt because it will save my life (a good). If I wear it because my mother told me to, or because it brings good luck, or because I just fancy doing so, or because it matched my shirt, I do the right thing but for the wrong reasons. If I don't wear it because I believe it will hinder my chances of survival in a car crash, then I do the wrong thing for the right reasons because I am in error. If I wear it because it will save my life, then I have comprehend the law and feel at home in it. At this point, there is no need for the law because the subject would legislate himself: it is what I want and what I want is justifiable as a reason for action that would be adopted, all things being equal, by everyone. Of course, laws are still required since subjects may need reminding of what is right and cannot be expected to continually rationalise what to do at every moment. They may even sometimes find a path of action too taxing to decide on their own.

RIGHT AND THE SHAPES OF FREEDOM (§§29–33)

The point of Hegel's introduction is to present his metaphysical description of freedom. An agent is free when he can endorse the end of his action as his own and be certain that it is the right course of action. Endorsement is a subjective attitude (homeliness) and certainty is gained by the attitudes of other agents belonging to our culture. Yet, is it possible to be at home in a culture where the dictates of right are not rational? Hegel would say no but he has to prove that to us. To put the problem in a slightly different and clearer way: how do we know that the limitations we apply to ourselves to purify our desires, the values of our society, are truly rational? Hegel's appeal to the social nature of reason giving opens his thesis up to the charge of relativism. His answer is opaque:

> *Right* is any existence in general which is the *existence* of the free will. Right is therefore in general freedom, as Idea. (§29)

A law is an objectified intention, that is an expression of a desire, preference or value on the part of the legislator.[9] A law is not merely coercion and a limitation on freedom, it can liberate: think of the laws for universal suffrage or compulsory education. These policies and laws increased the freedom of certain groups and individuals. Hegel holds that right is the externalisation of values which the individual self can justify to others so that they become objective, viz. motivations for all. A law then must embody motivations which an individual would endorse but the individual must also be able to endorse those laws that express rationality. This coming together of the objective and subjective is right but this right must develop from the abstract theorisations on metaphysical freedom we have begun with through the idea of externalisation (expression of desires), property, rights, action, morality and finally ethical life as a whole. The complex system of relationships is freedom because it frees us from the irrationality of brute drives and orders our desires via a system of immanent values, rights and duties. These taken together form the series of shapes of freedom.

How does one purify desire so it can become a basis for rational action? For Hegel the answer is to be found in the immanent relations of an individual to his or her state. The whole cohesive system of these relations will constitute the rational state. Social institutions, political establishments, economic organisations and domestic arrangements, religious movements and social units are to be understood as structures of thought and will. Institutions and other organisations are ways in which we understand ourselves and, as such, if they are not ones which make us independent, in the sense that we are at home in them and freely constrain ourselves by them, then they are not rational. These are the shapes of freedom in the modern state:

1. Abstract right: we understand ourselves as individual right-bearers, that is discrete atoms or persons who are independent from our nation, family and tribe;
2. Morality: we understand ourselves as autonomous moral subjects, responsible for our actions and demanding respect due to our standing;
3. Ethical life:
   a. Family: we understand ourselves as immediately associated with others through relationships based on love;
   b. Civil society: we understand ourselves as mediately associated with others through the media of work, class and exchange;
   c. The purely political state: we understand ourselves as mediately associated with others through the media of citizenship, institutional relationships and nationality.

Now, all we have to do is change this understanding (definitional work) into comprehension (the recognition of the actual form and requirements of these rational institutions) and also show how these various institutions can cohere harmoniously. That is the aim of Hegel's lecture series.

Study Questions

1. How does Hegel's account of free will differ from that of the British Empiricist tradition and what advantages does it have over such an account?
2. Why is arbitrariness essential to yet dangerous for human freedom?
3. What does 'purifying' one's desires involve?

CHAPTER 5

ABSTRACT RIGHT: PERSONAL FREEDOM

PREAMBLE

We have so far come to the position that the will has both a subjective and an objective aspect: subjectively, I can only act in such a way that I see the aim of my action as mine, as a purpose chosen by me; and, objectively, this purpose chosen by me cannot be arbitrary but must be rational, and the standard of rationality is the expectations, understandings and wills of others. Formally, we may understand what this means, but we shall not truly comprehend it until Hegel begins to put flesh on the bones. Part one of the *Philosophy of Right* is the first step of this incarnation: subjectively I represent myself as an atomistic self amongst other atomistic selves all pursuing wants, desires and projects. As selves, we intuitively understand ourselves as having – in some sense – a right to the unfettered and unhindered pursuit of these goals. Objectively, any society that hinders and obstructs unreasonably cannot be considered rational.

The subjective demand here rings a little familiar. It is very much the modern understanding of political societies: the idea of conflicting individual wills making demands on one another. Hobbes, at the very beginning of modernity, offered the new model of society as a necessary mediation between the conflicting interests of individuals (Hobbes, 1982). Yet, it would be a mistake to think that Hegel is in any way a part of this tradition. Abstract right, for him, is an essential element of a rational state but it is only the formal self-representation of the subject to himself and others as a rights-bearer. The idea of the bare person needs to be fleshed out by a substantial identity and a hierarchy of positive duties. Society is not a necessary evil (as it was for Hobbes) that constricts my freedom for the sake of peace, it is also the very substrate that makes freedom – in the Hegelian sense – possible.

So, the subjective demand would seem to require that for a state or community to be 'rational' (and this is now a term of art we shall use, following Hegel, to mean on one level legitimate or valid) it must ensure that the subject can recognise the end of his or her action as springing from internal motivations, as a good for him or her; that is, that my subjective desires, preferences and projects can be objectified in the world as an expression of who I am. That will be the subject matter of 'Morality', and in 'Ethical Life' Hegel will show that the state must also determine when said desires, preferences and projects cannot permissibly be satisfied and he will do so in terms of the rationality of such desires with reference to the objectified freedom of right in a specific community. However, the simplest way – and the intuitive way – to do so is to think of oneself as an individual with rights, as an individual with intrinsic worth whose desires, preferences and projects demand to be recognised as those of a person and not as the drives or instincts (or motion) of animals, children and objects. As such, the value of freedom dictates that we – as persons – be allowed to pursue these desires, preferences and projects. This is the realm of abstract right.

THE PERSON (§§34–40)

The person is Hegel's term of art for this atomistic, formal self in the pursuit of desires, projects and goals. The first part of the *Philosophy of Right* is an exploration of the idea of personal freedom. As a subject I am identified as that which brings something about in the world: the plant gives off oxygen, the lion roars, the human being plays cricket.[1] This subject is nothing but the identification of the origin of the change in the world. The human being, if he or she is a person, differs though. As a person, I am myself aware of me as bringing about this change: I buy, I steal, I desire and I can always relinquish the content of these desires. I somehow exist over and above them:

> The person is essentially different from the subject, for the subject is only the possibility of personality, since any living thing whatever is a subject. A person is therefore a subject which is aware of this subjectivity, for as a person, I am completely for

myself: the person is the individuality of freedom in pure being-for-itself. (§35A)

The person is both formal and universal: to be a person is to have the capacity to be the author of one's actions and, as such, it does not identify any specific subject nor make reference to any substantial content of the will.

When I ask myself who am I, I will give a list of characteristics that distinguish me from other things in the world: I am the father of Nicholas, I am a lecturer at Newcastle University, I am blond and so on. All of these facts constitute me as a specific existence, yet the person is what I am distinct from all of these, it is who 'I' am distinct from all those relationships which constitute 'me' (the family, the tribe, the nation, the job, etc.). It is akin to Patrick McGoohan's hollow cry at the beginning of the 1960s television programme *The Prisoner*: 'I am not a number, I am a free man.' I claim that I am something separate and independent from those roles and attributes which constitute my identity in full and that, over and above these, I deserve to be considered in virtue of some essential nature. And since this nature makes no reference to who I am substantially, it is a nature that all persons have and not just some. By expressing myself as a person, I claim rights and must confer similar rights on others.

To be a person on this model does not involve identifying specific interests (class, family, religion) but a demand for abstract right. Thus, the formal nature of personality is – oddly – universal differentiation. Hegel describes the person as 'inherently individual', and an 'exclusive individuality' (§34) and later as an 'atomic individuality' (§167). This is where political philosophy proper begins: if you have rights and so do I then we have territories and these territories may overlap and can be infringed. As an individual I have 'determinate ends' which I wish to express and actualise in the world through the satisfaction of my desires and preferences. This marks me out as a free individual. Abstract right is uninterested in the actual content of these desires (that is the realm of morality and ethics) but is interested in the claim that I – as person – have the right to express myself in the world; otherwise I would not be free. And so must you. And unfortunately, if the content of the will is undetermined, this will lead to conflict, whether it be conflict between two persons (wrong) or two subjects (morality) or between an individual and his family or his state (ethical life). The purpose of the element of abstract right is to lay the foundations for the rational resolution of such conflicts and that means we must ask which actions are permissible transgressions of rights and which are violations of rights.

In summary, personality is a universal status of equality. I cannot claim to be a person unless I confer this status on others: 'The commandment of right is therefore: *be a person and respect others as persons*' (§36). It is universal and entirely formal because it does not make reference to particular desires, interests or projects. In other words, it does not dictate what the content of these projects or interests ought to be. Instead it is constituted by the prohibition '*not to violate* personality and what ensues from personality' (§38). Abstract rights are only prohibitions and I cannot claim obligations on the part of others, since that requires a substantive social context. My parents or my state may *owe* me an education, but other abstract persons do not. To have obligations towards someone is to treat them in some sense as a particular person and not a formal universal rights-bearer. The realm of abstract right is, however, conceptually prior to positive social constructs of identity (even if it is historically posterior to them) since it is an expression of determinate individuality, of the individual *qua* individual. In order for me to have goods and constitute myself by social roles, I must first be able to freely choose such goods and pursue them without obstruction. If I cannot, then I am not free.

So, for Hegel, the person is a territory necessarily constituted by property which includes the rights to life and physical integrity (§48). I am a person and so I have the right – not just the possibility as an animal does – to fulfil my goals and projects. Property is the objective substrate that ensures this right is embodied in the state and this requires the institution of contract which determines my relations to others. As I am a person, then the demand for equality raises its head: you, too, are a person. I recognise you and you recognise me as a person through the establishment of contracts and legislated exchange and not through mere forceful taking and conferring. Actions are not events and a matter-of-fact account of how the stronger live off the weaker is an inappropriate description of the relations between persons. Consequently, the recognition of right and the legislation of exchange also acknowledges wrongdoing and requires punishment.

EQUALITY: A NORMATIVE CLAIM?

Before we look in detail at the substantive territory of the person in property, contract and wrongdoing, alert readers will have noticed what appears to be Hegel's first normative claim: a rational state is one characterised by the existence of persons as opposed to subjects and personality is only possible in a community of equals. In other words, the society which ensures and maintains equality amongst citizens is a good society. Given what we said in the second chapter about the critical ambition of Hegel's work, it would be fruitful to ask some questions: How does Hegel justify the claim to equality? And, what (if any) normative commitments arise from such a claim?

In order to justify the norm of equality, it will be pertinent to remind ourselves of Hegel's philosophical position.[2] Due to his idealism, he believes that knowledge about the world can only be the self-knowledge of spirit. Judgements are made within the context of rational understanding and so one must recognise that reason imposes itself on the world. Hegel inaugurates the transition from the subject–object relation of knowledge to a subject–subject relation since I can only be certain of my judgements if they meet the standards of reasoning of other subjects. My judgements require validation by another. In the realm of right, the subject firstly demands to know how he can be certain that he is different from animals and does in fact act on his own will as opposed to external necessity. The answer is once more through the validation of others: I must be sure that they are aware of me as free and I am aware of them as free and this certainty is gained through interpersonal understanding characterised as communal mind: 'this absolute substance which is the unity of the different independent self-consciousnesses which, in their opposition, enjoy perfect freedom and independence: "I" that is "We" and "We" that is "I" ' (PhG, ¶177).

Much has been written on Hegel's dialectic of lordship and bondage, and it has been used in many different contexts, but I shall limit myself to what is of interest here and as such I shall return to one of the earlier readings. Kojève grounds the need for recognition in the desire for the self to demonstrate his freedom: 'For man to be truly human, for him to be essentially and really different from an animal, his human Desire must actually win out over his animal

Figure 1   © AP/EMPICS

Desire' (Kojève, 1969, 6). In the dialectic, Hegel gives us one way to do this: 'And it is only through staking one's life that freedom is won' (PhG, ¶187). What is the role of staking one's life here?

I always remember the image of a protestor in Tiananmen Square (figure 1) which shows him standing before a column of tanks. This has always seemed to me to raise the greatest problem posed to a Hobbesian (or any naturalist) account of motivation. The man is prepared to sacrifice his life in the pursuit of an ideal (liberty, equality) that is never going to be enjoyed by himself. The desire for self-preservation, supposedly the strongest in our storehouse of desires, is trumped by an abstract and formal value which if you asked the man exactly what he wanted, what equality and liberty will actually be if he is successful in attaining them, he would find it nigh on impossible to articulate. But, he is prepared to stake his life for the sake of a principle. We are left in no doubt that this is a human being and not an animal.

Of course, the man's actions would not be interpreted as human action, as a demonstration of his freedom, unless there were others around him able to understand his sacrifice. In his case, he appeals to the tank driver, the Chinese government and, perhaps, the global mass media's audience. The watching dog would not be able to see this as a relinquishment of desires. (Please do not look for the dog in the image. In a mistaken response to a bureaucratic dictate, it was airbrushed out.) His actions require other free subjects to acknowledge them as a free act, otherwise they are meaningless. The theory of recognition offers an alternative to Hobbesian social atomism: the idea that society arises due to fear and dependence and from the need to mediate between conflicts of individual wills. Rather, society arises out of the desire for inter-subjective recognition since this makes freedom possible.[3]

In Hegel's story, the demonstration of one's freedom is by the same staking of one's life, but in the beginning the meeting between two self-consciousnesses results in a struggle to the death. If one cedes or dies and becomes a slave or corpse, then he is not a person (he is like a dog) and cannot confer personality on the other. The resolution requires mutual recognition. This mutual recognition is a product of a drawn-out historical development that we do not have time to follow (but will say a little about later on in this book). Within rational society, as we shall see, property, marriage and the other elements of ethical life provide an alternative way to demonstrate my humanity and hence are necessary for full human freedom.

The moral of the story is that if I claim to be a person with rights, I require other persons with rights otherwise I am not sure of myself. The concept of the person is the first objective embodiment of this requirement of recognition in a political state. Personality has to be mutual because it is a universal concept. I can only claim to be a person if I also recognise those who do not violate my rights as persons. Equality, the moral ascription of the right to satisfy one's desires, stretches to all persons. Without this recognition there are no persons, and I am not a person: 'Self-consciousness exists in and for itself when, and by that fact that, it so exists for another; that is, it exists only in being acknowledged' (PhG, ¶178).

THE NORMATIVE COMMITMENTS OF EQUALITY

Does this mean Hegel can make the evaluative judgement that a society characterised by the moral norm of equality is better than one which is not (in his words, is more rational)? The simple answer is yes. The normative claim amounts to this: any society which has an institution of slavery is not rational, neither is one that does not – in whatever way – acknowledge equality between persons. Yet, these norms are hard-won conclusions to a history of struggle (§§274A and 331R). The emergence of the person is an historical event and, Hegel holds, a people at an earlier stage of history would not have had personality. The person comes about only through mutual recognition.[4] And to be free, a people must experience this history for themselves:

> If we hold firmly to the view that the human being in and for himself is free, we thereby condemn slavery. But if someone is a slave, his own will is responsible, just as the responsibility lies with the will of a people if that people is subjugated. Thus the wrong of slavery is the fault not only of those who enslave or subjugate people, but of the slaves and the subjugated themselves. Slavery occurs in the transitional phase between natural human existence and the truly ethical condition; it occurs in a world where a wrong is still right. Here, the wrong is *valid*, so that the position it occupies is a necessary one. (§57A)

How can a slave be responsible for his own serfdom? If we free them, then this is an act of external causality. The slave alone is capable of freeing himself since to not be a slave is to act on one's own will – it cannot be done from outwith. Slavery is the imposition of external determination on the will. Slaves should be freed like children, through development, and this leaves them at the mercy of history. Slaves are freed when the idea of a person emerges and establishes itself as a political notion. For Hegel, one cannot export the values of liberalism (or even the dictates of the realm of abstract right) to other nations because to prescribe how others ought to behave may increase their well-being, but it leaves them as enchained as before. They merely swap one authority for another and remain unfree (§65).

Now, this might have some horrible consequences: we can't interfere in the development of cultures, they should work their ways through history for themselves. So, we may rightly judge human sacrifice to be wrong, but we cannot impose a law externally on a culture which is out of joint with its time. It is only in mature states that religions which violate personal rights become intolerable (§270R). Again, remember that for Hegel we are all children of our time and as such we can only work over what is intuitive and immediate to us.

History itself is the ultimate arbiter of rationality. It also may promote treating 'primitives' like children, but we shall discuss these consequences when we look at world history at the close of this book. Yet, more pressingly, Hegel has to face a problem. In Rousseau, mutual recognition is guaranteed by equality in a homogeneous state which is classless. In this way, there can be no 'us' against 'them' and I feel at home with my peers. Hegel, however, celebrates class difference and separate interests. How, then, can equality be ensured and what exactly does the norm substantively demand? Property is one answer to that.

PROPERTY (§§41–71) AND CONTRACT (§§72–81)

The explanation or justification of property can take various forms: (i) Rousseau tells us it is an ideological con trick; (ii) Locke tells us it is a natural right; (iii) he also adds it is deserved; (iv) Freud holds it is necessary for the satisfaction of needs in a social group; (v) and Kant holds it is what all rational agents would agree to if they reasoned. Hegel differs radically from these traditional and intuitive answers to the justification of property. For him, property is the rational existence of a person and the expression (the objectification) of particular personality and territory. The ground of Hegel's justification of the institution of private property lies (and although it should not surprise us, it should strike us as radical, daring and odd) in freedom.

The subjective will must be recognised as freedom, so it requires the institution of property to differentiate the 'instinctual taking' of the animal from the 'rational appropriation' of the human being (§§45–46, 51). Without the conventions and expectations of property none of this would be possible. One way to understand this demand for equality of persons through property is made clear from an earlier version of his lectures:

> The *essential being* of ownership is the *determinate existence* of its right-governed absolute aspect, namely that in ownership persons *recognize* one another as persons. This means that in the consciousness of their self-identity they know themselves to be identical with others through the mediation of external existence, and they accept one another as mutually free and independent. (FPR, §31)

Property is a medium though which the embodiment of the will is manifest; we fashion a world which expresses our difference and discreteness in 'an external *sphere of freedom*' (§41). Personality requires property in order to demonstrate its particularity to the world: I assert myself as a free individual through the appropriation of the objects of my desires and wants. The substrate of property is 'external' in that it is separate from my will and must be so in order to maintain and promote the freedom of that will.

How does property – and more specifically the institution of private property – maintain and promote personal freedom? The first response is simple: an autonomous life is one in which the individual is self-determined and this means choosing one's life plan from a rational system of goods. The expression of me as a person requires a system of property through which I can acquire goods, exchange goods and choose amongst goods. Property – Hegel assumes private – frees me from the dependence of day-to-day living. If I am working simply to feed my family and survive, I will not be capable of making any free choices about the way in which I want to live my life as I am subject to external necessity. A system of private property generates enough surplus wealth so that I am freed from the necessity of needs. In simple parlance, the idea is that property 'increases' my freedom, though Hegel does not mean this just in the facile sense of I can afford to do more things if I am rich.

However, any system of property, a common one for example (the village green is an instance of common property, as we all have an inclusive right to use it), will free me from the necessity of needs. Some communal villages with a division of labour into specialisms and cooperation would be able, perhaps, to generate leisure time for individuals and also a system of goods to choose amongst. Hegel has argued that property, the production and distribution of goods, is necessary for freedom, but not private property. He, however, openly states that common property does not and cannot express the appropriate relationship between the person and external things. The person requires the social possibility to act on the arbitrary will, to act on whatever the content of one's will happens to be, and common property (including extended family rights) constrain the territory within which one can act arbitrarily and contingently (§46). Hegel would say that any form of common property will make the expression of me as a discrete and independent person impossible. Private property introduces boundaries and territories that support the realm of personal freedom, the realm of abstract right, in a way a system of common property could not. I can decide what to do with my property, which property to acquire, and this expresses my values and hence my personal freedom separate from and independent of the family, the state or community:

> In relation to external things, the *rational* aspect is that I possess property; the *particular* aspect, however, includes subjective ends, needs, arbitrariness, talents, external circumstances, etc. . . . *What* and *how much* I possess is therefore purely contingent as far as right is concerned. (§49)

And this is important because the relation between the person and the world is expressed through what he needs, uses and alienates. Of course, one consideration immediately arises: it cannot be wholly arbitrary *how much* one possess since if property is fundamental to personal freedom, then all persons 'ought to have property' as Hegel acknowledges in the addition, but we shall discuss this when we look at poverty within civil society later on (§§240–45). The discussion of recognition and equality has given us a basis for the modern ethical prescription of equality and it is obvious that propertyless persons have a diminished moral status. Poverty reduces man to living a life determined once more by the necessity of needs and they are ripe to be exploited: others, wealthy people, can treat them as tools or instruments for their own satisfaction rather than respect them as persons. Does that mean property ought to be equally distributed? The answer is of course no, because my personality is bounded and inviolable, so the state cannot wholly dictate what I must do with my property and how much I ought to own. For Hegel, private property follows on from the formal demand for equality (respect persons as equal), but it does not necessarily entail substantial, distributive equality. Such patterned distribution of goods would contradict the personal freedom – the choice to buy what I want, to spend my money how I wish – that private property seeks to facilitate.

So, private property, not common property will mark my distinctiveness as a person and facilitate self-understanding (§49). Hegel believes different social ways of life allow greater freedom, and that progress has been made from the idea of man as a member of a tribe whose goods were identical with and determined by the collective good to the atomistic person, who possesses individual goods expressing his own particularity. And here we see why property is an abstract right: it sets up the territory around the person that cannot be violated by others or by state decisions. Rights, after all, are normally justified by the private versus public decision: what part of my life do I have control over and what part does the state decide. The state, on this model, cannot violate the rights of life, liberty and property or, put more simply, it cannot decide whether I live or die, what I do with my life and how I express myself (§49).[5] All of these must be personal decisions if I am to be free. And this is the ultimate justification of abstract right: freedom. Without the realm of abstract right, human beings cannot become fully free. The rights are objectified through property, recognised through contract and affirmed through the reaction to wrongdoing. The boundary of abstract right is set by prohibition and, on the level of abstract right, no positive rights (to education, for example) can be claimed since these belong to the determinations of the ethical state and not abstract right. These are goods which have been decided to be rational and worth promoting. Abstract right remains on the level of contingency: these are my goods and I affirm them as a particular ego.

The actualising of the inner will through property takes three forms: appropriation (seizure, artifice/creation; marking with a sign); using (consumption); alienation (the idea that if something is mine as opposed to being a mere means to the satisfaction of a desire or a need, I have the capacity to relinquish my ownership of it). I need not consume it, I can exchange it, bequeath it or sell it. This truly distinguishes an institution of property from mere consumption and this requires contract.[6] Exchange concerns the volition of two wills; it is a response to how and when someone or something can impinge my territory and it is based once more on the relationship of mutual recognition: consent can be given to adults, one either punishes or tolerates children. For Hegel, one cannot sell something to an animal or a child, but only to those things in the world recognised as persons. Only persons are able to exchange, bequeath and buy (§74). Such a claim may sound absurd, but when the child offers me money for an object, there is no true sense of the value of what he wants or what he is exchanging for it and such a relationship is one of playful condescension on the part of the adult and not equality.

Property is, then, one of those rights that give me the moral status of a person, making people identify me as an individual and respect my liberty as an individual rather than just a member of the tribe. Agents are free to become what they choose and they can only understand that when they have achieved certain goals. Property is a sign of what I have made of myself and also a communication of myself, what I am, to others. The clothes make the man, so to speak. What I choose to buy (Elizabeth Duke jewellery), wear (a hooded shell-suit) and drive (a souped-up Fiesta) tell a story about who I am and how I see myself. Similarly, I can learn about myself from the expression of my tastes through the system of private property. Yes, I am a father, but I am also the father who wears this and drives that. Private property allows me to see who I am and I suppose change it: just as I am the one who wants to flee the scene of the cat's dying (see chapter 4), but also wants to want to put it out of its misery, so I might be the one who wants to buy a novel by Jeffrey Archer, but wants to want to buy one by Gabriel García Márquez. The objective freedom of private property allows the subjective freedom of rational determination and the purification of one's drives in a way that common property would not. It is not the mere satisfaction of needs but a system of communication that allows free beings to mark out their distinctiveness and to bring them to an understanding of themselves. Hegel's justification of the system of property rights then has very little to do with external necessity or needs: 'In relation to needs – if these are taken as primary – the possession of property appears as a means; but the true position is that, from the point of view of freedom, property, as the first *existence* of freedom, is an essential end for itself' (§45R; see also 41A). It allows persons to purify their desires and to properly be a person. There are, of course, other ways to communicate who I am to others, or to understand what I have achieved, than private property, but private property, Hegel argues, is a necessary element of this communication.

WRONG (§§82–99)

Necessarily, when there are rights, there will be illegitimate violations of these rights and that is wrong. It is no longer the description that 'It happened' but the evaluation that 'It should not have happened' which begins to characterise human beings' appraisal of one another. Wrong, for Hegel, is a 'semblance' of right, by which he means: 'an opposition between right in itself and the particular will as that in which right becomes a *particular right*' (§82). By becoming a 'particular right', the formal universal nature of abstract right is lost and so is the substrate which guarantees personal freedom. In other words, without the notion of wrong and punishment, my personal freedom cannot be assured. Hegel begins by listing the different types of wrong.

First, there is wrongdoing which is unintentional or non-malicious. Two persons may, for example, claim the same object and so they are in agreement about rights and the rules of property distribution, but one or both of them are mistaken about some fact of the matter. Such a situation is a mere collision of individual wills and, although there is agreement on right, the conflict generally concerns whether a violation has occurred or not.

Second, if I sell you a pair of shoes from the market, but you get home to find a brick in the shoebox, then this is a case of deception. I simply do not recognise the universality of the contract, believing myself to be exempt from it yet willing – at the same time – that it applies to everyone else. Although the criminal recognises the rules governing property transactions, the wrongdoing consists in the need for the victim to abide by the rules and to earnestly believe that I, the criminal, do so too.

Third, coercion and crime consists in denying the victim's rights as a person and negating their deserved status. Coercion, like slavery, involves equal parts of responsibility and bad faith for Hegel: 'Only he who *wills* to be *coerced* can be coerced into anything' (§91). If I put a gun to your head and demand your wallet, your strongest desire is to preserve your life, but you should still acknowledge the pull of your conscience not to give me the money and this for Hegel means that there still exists a choice. The will of the criminal seeks to destroy the 'personality' of the victim and his free choice by trumping his free will with external necessity.

Perhaps we need to ask whether there is any substantial difference between the second and third types. If we were a Kantian, we might say both involve using the other as a mere means and this is basically what is at stake for Hegel. Although, unlike Kant, treating others not as persons cannot be the be all and end all of moral or legal action. Abstract right is the first and most simple account of the sphere of freedom of the person in the modern state. In deception, we make ourselves an exception: all should obey the law so that I and my interests can profit. In coercion, the other becomes a tool for the purpose of fulfilling my ends and I therefore negate any right he has to consent or withhold from my action. In both cases, the criminal has to recognise the realm of right and also to will it (it is required for the success of his aims), yet he negates it through violation: either through the deception or non-recognition of others.

The actions of the criminal undermine the regime and system of right. If I were to steal something and get away with it, then what I have stolen would become mine. This is a new way to have property, but it is inimical to personal freedom. Since the very nature of property is to facilitate the expression of personal freedom, then this kind of property acquisition undermines that end. It is irrational and, as such, the rules of right that make personal freedom possible would no longer be valid. Yet, this is equally true of both deception and crime proper. The real difference lies in the self-consciousness of the criminal and the severity of the criminal's irrationality: 'The difference between crime and deception is that in the latter, a recognition of right is still present in the form of the action, and this is correspondingly absent in the case of crime' (§83A). Deception requires recognition of right and free will since in order to deceive someone the victim has to make a free choice. Coercion, however, is conceptually wrong because in using others as means, I recognise that they are persons (otherwise I would not be able to use them as means, they would be a tool) but simultaneously negate their status as a person: '. . . force or coercion immediately destroys itself in its concept, since it is the expression of a will which cancels the expression or existence of a will. Force or coercion, taken in the abstract, is *contrary to right*' (§92). By putting a gun to someone's head, I acknowledge that they have free will and the possibility to say 'No' to my demand, but – at the same time – I attempt to make it impossible for them to say 'No', to reduce them to the level of external necessity. Wrongdoing is a challenge to the system of right and this system makes our freedom possible. Rationality demands that these structures of freedom be protected and that protection is effected through punishment.

PUNISHMENT (§§100–4)

Here is the problem with punishment. On any account of punishment, actions will involve a violation of rights (liberty, property, physical integrity) through incarceration, privation or corporal harm. All such actions are, of course, wrong in most sensible moral codes. Punishment, at bottom, seems to be a two-wrongs-make-a-right and that is something my mother has always told me is wrong. It is, however, the missing part of Hegel's doctrine of abstract right: with wrongdoing, a person denies the validity of right and reduces the system of rights to a mere 'semblance' and these rights need to be enforceable if they are to be effective. To be effective, rights must maintain and promote the freedom of the individual. Punishment enforces the system of rights.

Hegel's justification of punishment seems to work on two levels: one, punishment is necessary for the system of rights to be effective and if they are not effective there is no personal freedom, so punishment is rational; and two, if punishments are not to be further violations of rights, then he needs a story to say how a criminal consents to his punishments and to therefore show that no violation has occurred. The first of these justifications is implicit in the lectures (and follows a familiar course if you look back over what we have said about property), whereas the second is explicit and controversial (Wood, 1990, chap. 6; Houlgate, 1992; Wood, 1992).

So, let us quickly go over the idea that effective rights entail punishment. We suggested above that if I were to steal a car and get away with it, then I invalidate the system of rights and this demands that I am denounced or punished. It demands that the nature of my wrongdoing is made objective, otherwise the system of rights which supports and makes possible personal freedom no longer serves its purpose. So, for example, having laws against soft-drug taking, if these are not enforced legally or even through public opinion, is tantamount to there being no such laws. Punishment is about enforcing rights.

Now, we ought to be careful this is not understood as a simple deterrent account of punishment and this is where the justification of punishment moves from the implicit justification to the explicit one. Punishment is about what is recognised as right and wrong within a community. In Locke's state of nature, criminals lose their status as persons: when someone violates natural rights they are no different from a rabid animal and are to be treated as a danger to the community. Just as animals are not right-bearers, neither are criminals (Locke, 1988, chap. 2). Yet, it follows from this that even the most minor crimes can be greeted with the death penalty (the criminal loses all rights, including the right to life). And the most severe and barbaric punishments may, just as a matter of fact, be the greatest deterrents. Hegel has an opposite view: any form of punishment which acts as a deterrent, as a coercive prevention, as a rehabilitation of the criminal or as a good for society as a whole may well be useful but such utility cannot be the *justification* since it does not allow subjects the chance to express their freedom (§99A). And it is the very humanity of the criminal which demands his or her punishment. The criminal has a right to punishment (§100). Persons have to be aware that they are responsible and ought to be treated as such since their action expresses their own particularity. We fail to honour the criminal as a rational being if we do not punish him or her. If I do not punish you for slapping me in the face, I ignore you as I would a boisterous small child or a leaf blown by the wind. So, I treat you as a thing or as an non-rational being and – as such – I violate your personality. It is wrong not to punish and you merit and deserve it and so does the system of rights itself.

So, given Hegel's position on freedom, punishment can neither be justified as a deterrent nor as a form of rehabilitation, since neither do justice to the 'honour' of the criminal or the expression of his or her will in the action of wrongdoing. Traditionally, that leaves only one justification of punishment left and it is the one which Hegel endorses: retributivism. The criminal is punished because he or she *deserves* it. Intuitively we understand this as a desire for revenge: when I am wronged, I seek recompense and Hegel hints at how this a-rational desire develops into the rational system of justice because punishments need to be codified and 'agreed upon', hence the need for it to be taken out of the hands of the victims or particular wills, otherwise the criminal may not recognise his punishment as just. If I kill a man for apple scrumping, his family have a legitimate claim against me for overreaction. Similarly, if judgements concerning punishments are left in the hands of the individual wills, then partiality will undermine the aims of a system of rights. Particular individuals' decisions for recompense will be arbitrary, being either too lenient or too harsh, and new claims will be made, in return, on the behalf of others:

> Thus revenge, as the positive action of a *particular* will, becomes a *new infringement*; because of this contradiction, it becomes part of an infinite progression and is inherited indefinitely from generation to generation. (§102)[7]

Arbitrariness in punishment leads to vendetta and the system of rights is once more undermined.

How then do we determine proper and appropriate punishments? On the one hand, this is not a philosophical concern. The nature of abstract right and the demand for punishment does not determine the form or codes of punishment: the existing state already has a system of punishments which we recognise as such. The actual codification is a social product and not a matter of philosophical concern; it should meet only the formal claim of proportionality and common sense: more serious crimes are to be punished more stringently. The substantial understanding of how and how much is left up to a specific society and its history and a system of justice is accountable to public opinion alone (§218R). On the other hand, though, punishment becomes a concern of morality: the criminal demands to be punished otherwise we treat him as an animal or a child. Such a stance exhibits a strong Kantian strain, hence the movement to morality; it concerns the subjectivity of the will, but this means the criminal is responsible for his action and recognises this responsibility. Punishment therefore requires the idea of intentional action and individual moral law. Abstract right is incomplete to deal with the actual codification of crimes and their punishments and can only be completed by the explanation how, when and by what degree we are responsible for our actions (a theory of action) and what we ought or ought not to be doing (a doctrine of duties). The discussion requires an exposition of morality.

THE TRANSITION TO MORALITY

The bottom line is that punishment is necessary for a system of rights to be effective and, hence, for right-abiding individuals. Yet, it does require that punishments need to be codified by an external authority which individuals recognise as an authority. In abstract right, the content of will is given: I want this, I need that, and the nature of right is to justify these claims and set boundaries amongst individuals. But, if I have not chosen my desires, then it is very hard to say I am fully responsible for them (only a Humean compatibility picture seems relevant and that would lead to a completely different discussion of punishment in terms of deterrence and character manipulation). Thus, the theory of punishment Hegel offers is incomplete without a discussion of responsibility: because if your action demands to be treated as a human action, then you must have chosen your purpose and see it as a good. If not, I treat you like a dog. Such a claim requires a discussion of intentions and responsibility. When I make my needs and wants into an object – when I conceive of myself as 'a person wanting this or that' – then I become an object for myself. And to say whether it is *good* to want this or that (not just *right*) is to evaluate my wants and needs. And evaluation is the realm of the subjective will and the moral point of view.

Study Questions

1. Does it make sense to say that certain 'individuals and peoples do not yet have personality' (§35R)? Is such an assertion true, merely distasteful or politically dangerous?
2. Are the institutions of capitalism and private property inimical to or favourable for human freedom? What is Hegel's position and is it convincing?
3. Is poverty a moral or a pragmatic problem for Hegel?

CHAPTER 6

MORALITY: MORAL FREEDOM

PREAMBLE

'Morality', part two of the *Philosophy of Right*, bridges the sections 'Abstract Right' and 'Ethical Life [*Sittlichkeit*]'. The former section, as we have seen, is concerned with the rights and prohibitions of the discrete self as differentiated from the clan or the tribe; claims which involve recognition by others and identification of others as liberal, atomistic selves with particular desires. Such basic subjective freedom ('I want x') would not be able to posit and desire its own particular end without the prohibitions and rights entailed by the emergence of the *person* as distinct from the tribe. The latter section, 'Ethical Life', is concerned with the positive duties and obligations of the citizen in the rational state: the good-for-me and the good-for-all of the rational social being have to be purified and harmonised by positive obligations entailed by and arising from the subject's various roles in ethical life.

'Morality' concerns the transition from prohibition to obligation, from *person* to *moral subject*, in such a way as to guarantee that the limitations imposed on one's will are those in which one can feel *at home* (§105; see also EG, §503). With the person, rights enable or obstruct the satisfaction of subjective freedom and law determines the claims of individuals within a group made effective by punishment. However, the subjective freedom of the person is merely in itself, an external purpose imposed on him, be it by immediate inclination or blind obedience to the dictates of authority. In part two of the *Philosophy of Right*, we find the Hegel who is most consistent with the Enlightenment, since he sees the Enlightenment as the epoch of reason and reason which must be demonstrated to the individual. Hegel is here expressing certain intimate themes of post-Reformation Europe: just as the priest no longer mediates my relationship with God, neither do experts, nor teachers, nor men in power mediate my relationship with reasons for action. When a pharaoh wanted a pyramid built, it was enough for all other Egyptians that he had asked since he was divine. When the Greeks set out for Troy, it was enough for Agamemnon to demand the loyal allegiance of his subjects because he was their king. But, to secure the allegiance of other kings, he had to demonstrate the 'just' nature of his cause and the opportunity for glory (a good for them). The Enlightenment now demands that the rationality of any dictate from authority be demonstrated to each individual as all are now free (the equality of personhood): 'The East knew and to the present day knows only that *One* is Free; the Greek and Roman world, that *some* are free; the German World knows that *All* are free' (VPG, 104).

The demonstration of the rationality of a dictate from authority can appeal to values or to reasons, but may just be the answer to the simple question: what's in it for me? It is the subject's intention, which reflects an inwardness as opposed to the external nature of the person, that is most readily named freedom:

> This subjective or 'moral' freedom is what a European especially calls freedom. In virtue of the right thereto a man must possess a personal knowledge of the distinction between good and evil in general: ethical and religious principles shall not merely lay their claim on him as external laws and precepts of authority to be obeyed, but have their assent, recognition, or even justification in his heart, sentiment, conscience, intelligence, etc. The subjectivity of the will in itself is its supreme aim and absolutely essential to it. (EG, §503)

The will which obeys authority or immediate inclination acts only in itself, it is not aware of the rationality of purpose. That is the will of the mere person. The moral subject instead transcends and interrogates the content of his will, asking if the 'I want x' is a good-for-him and, if he perceives it so, he claims *responsibility* for the purpose as his *own*. Hegel, in the above quotation, celebrates this modern, moral freedom; it is, for him, necessary for full, human freedom and any ethical substance which did not recognise and value it would be incomplete and not therefore rational.

HEGEL'S THEORY OF ACTION (§§105–28)

A while ago I remember a debate concerning the danger of playing heavy metal records backwards since, it was claimed, they included messages from the Devil or coded instructions for adolescents to commit suicide or instigate revolution. Putting aside my incredulity in the belief that there ever was a Satan-inspired rock conspiracy (I must admit once trying, but having to stop as I was too worried about scratching the vinyl – one wonders if angels gave us the CD to avert the Apocalypse), we can use this as an example if we suspend our disbelief for a moment. Let us say that Randy from Milwaukee listens to Iron Maiden or Judas Priest and there are in fact messages that affect in him the desire to commit suicide. The operation is akin to hypnosis or indoctrination of the *Clockwork Orange* kind. As he puts the gun to his head, let us ask a simple question: is he free?

The empirical British tradition, originating in Hobbes, would say something as brutally obvious as this: Randy is free if he is able to fulfil his desire (Hobbes, 1982, chap. 21). Coercion, threats and hypnosis merely alter the desirability of our doing one thing over another and have no effect on our freedom. Freedom is freedom to do. There seems to be something amiss here. Randy is free in one sense because the desire can either be satisfied or not; we could tie him up or not leave a gun lying around and so on. Yet, this is the freedom of abstract right where the content of the will is given. But there is a further question concerning whether or not Randy is responsible for what he does and this question presupposes a different conception of freedom. And Hegel has shown us that punishment, as he conceives it, demands this other conception of freedom. At the most basic level, we could say that the agent acts on his own desires when he sees the end as a good for him, in other words that – if he were to reflect on his action – he would intend to do it. Freedom is freedom to choose to do or not to do. It is considerations such as these that allow us to treat adults differently from children, career thieves from kleptomaniacs and – to a certain extent – murderers from psychotics. (The difference can be understood, according to Hegel, as the intuition that the former of each pair all demand 'respect' for their crime whereas the latter are probably good objects for deterrent and rehabilitative practices, although we should not call this punishment because one can only punish the rational agent.)

So, punishment – unsurprisingly – rests upon an understanding of action, after all we hold people responsible for what they do. This may sound like a truism: if my father were serving thirty years in prison and he died after ten, I would be put out if the court demanded the debt of twenty years from me, since 'I did nothing'. Yet, there are more important considerations in this distinction between an action and a happening or an event: when is it a murderous shooting and when a hunting accident as often happens to vice-presidents? Abstract right, since it is concerned with the person as formal rights-bearer, is unable to help us when we attempt to understand the particular case of crime or of wrongdoing. In order to rationalise our practices of crime and punishment, we need to treat the human being as a moral subject and not as a mere person by looking at his or her intentions. The moral subject is not only prohibited from acting in certain ways, he is also obliged *by himself* to act in certain ways and the will is no longer merely in-itself because he reflects on it: the reason becomes known to the agent and is for-itself rational. A child looks both ways before crossing the road because his mother tells him to (the action is rational in-itself), but when he is an adult he looks both ways before crossing the road whether his mother tells him to or not and understands why (the action is rational for-him). As such, the intention becomes something inward, the content of the will is transcended and questioned: is this good for me? Hegel puts it thus: 'Only in the will as subjective will can freedom, or the will which has being *in itself*, be actual' (§106). So, the moral will is necessary for full human freedom and a rational state must maintain and promote it. The section entitled 'Morality' describes what the moral will is and what it requires and it shows how it is only possible given an immanent doctrine of duties, or ethical life. The inwardness of the moral will involves the agent in relations with others, for in acting upon a reason for itself, the subject seeks recognition in the externality of his will; which is to say, his action is intended to reflect the positive content of his purpose and be recognised by others as 'good'.

Hegel separates the deed from the action. In acting on the world, I bring about a chain of events which originate in my action. Some of these are deliberate and some are not. How do we know what the subject is responsible for? If the deed is the alteration in the external world brought about by the will, the action is that part of the deed for which the subject can claim responsibility. These two are, of

course, not identical: in opening a door in ignorance and accidentally knocking the decorator off his ladder, the subject is only
responsible for actually opening the door. His deed may have been
to knock over the decorator, but his action was to open the door. A
proviso should be added in that the right of the intention has an
objectivity which holds that the action must include knowledge
which the agent *should* know. Thus, the arsonist who says he only
wanted to light one blade of grass is responsible for the destruction
of the field, because he *should have known* that it was a likely
outcome, and if the man opens the door, he ought to do so carefully
if he has the decorators in (§119A). And, when the Vice-president
shoots his friend and states, 'I didn't mean to, it was just an accident',
we need to be able to say that – since it was not a good for the Vice-
president that his friend died – then his description of the event is
accurate. For the most part, first-person accounts of actions will be
reliable.

How does this help us with the problematic cases of brainwashed,
hypnotised and coerced agents? If a purpose is not *recognised* internally by the agent, then it cannot be the free will of a subject and this
consideration rules out external factors such as deep unconscious
motivations, the precepts of authority or, more strongly, acting to
save one's life in face of a threat or natural causality. These all serve
to explain an action, but they do not necessarily make the agent
responsible for the act. For Hegel, only when the subject is recognised as responsible for his or her act (as the external expression of
intention) is he or she fully free. Obviously, then, he has to characterise the way in which subjects are held responsible for their actions
and this means offering a description of intentional action.

Hegel starts with a formal point: the change in the world for which
the subject is responsible is that to which the predicate 'mine' can be
attached (§115). The coerced or hypnotised agent would probably
say, on viewing what they had done at a later date, 'That was not me.
I did not, would not, want to do that.' As such, they cannot recognise the action as their own and it is easy for us to see that, when the
bank robber holds a gun to the teller, the teller may *want* to put the
money in the bag, but only in so far as the will of the bank robber is
expressed through the teller. Thus, the act can be described in terms
of a purpose (the particular will's cognisance of an external principle in terms of an internal motivation such as *fear*, in this example
the bank teller's purpose is not to be shot) but it is made more

specific in terms of an intention (the universal intelligibility which others will understand in my act; the teller will only be free if he, too, wants the robber to have the money and would have handed it over even without the presence of a gun). Purpose is proper to the description of *persons*, of children and animals, but moral subjects require the more specific language of intentions:

> Purpose concerns only the formal condition that the external will should also be present within me as an internal element. In the second moment, on the other hand, the question arises of the intention behind the action – that is, of the relative value of the action in relation to me. (§114A)

To describe an occurrence as an action for which the agent is fully responsible, it is not enough that one can recognise a motivation in a specific agent, but that motivation must be the agent's own. The foundations of subjective responsibility are described in a crucial paragraph:

> The expression of the will as *subjective* or *moral* is *action*. Action contains the following determinations: (α) it must be known by me in its externality as mine; (β) its essential relation to the concept is one of obligation; and (γ) it has an essential relation to the will of others. (§113)

(α) The first of these criteria demands a *right of knowledge*: the intention of the agent must be known to the agent himself. Hegel argues that to act from a given, immediate or natural reason is not an actualisation of freedom, the agent must recognise in his action the end to which it is projected; thus agents who act from deep psychoses, hypnosis or external determinations (or as Hegel terms them 'children, imbeciles, lunatics') do not act freely (§120R). This element emphasises the first-person priority of the knowledge of an act in that the subject of the moral will (not necessarily the person, though) has the best access to his intentions. For it is the moral will, in contrast to the simple desiring will, which has authority over its actions. Hegel elsewhere describes the moral will as 'inviolable' and 'inaccessible'; that is, the subject is privileged in his description of his purpose and should not be contradicted unless it is absolutely necessary (§106A).[1] The moral point of view forms the basis of *subjective freedom*: 'The agent has no less the right to see that the particularity of content in the action, in point of its matter, is not something external to him, but is a particularity of his own – that it contains his needs, interests, and aims' (EG, §505). The intention of the agent is his own well-being, so a normative 'ought' arises from the very nature of intention: this is a reason for me in that it is my 'good'. (A good, one should stress, which is not exclusively moral in nature; it can be self-regarding, prudential, etc.) Therefore, the subject only claims responsibility for those acts in which he satisfies his own free desires, projects and aspirations.

(β) Second, action demonstrates the subject's essential humanity in that, holding the end to be a binding good, he posits an external relationship to it of obligation or duty. The animal has no choice but to obey its desires, and neither does the small child; they bear little responsibility for their actions. Subjective freedom for them – and to a similar extent for the *person* of abstract right – resides in the satisfaction of the will's desire whatever its content may be. With fully developed subjects, values override other desires and they recognise that the external ends of actions belong necessarily to themselves. Values are not to be understood in opposition to desires; rather they are the articulation of desires which the subject believes are worth having. Neither, once again, need these values be exclusively moral; responsibility also concerns self-regarding actions (self-interest and prudence). Willing of this sort, as we shall see, is necessary for civil society, thus it cannot be exclusively moral. Duties, then, can also be prudential (I ought to take out a pension plan) and self-interested (I ought to buy this because I like it). The judgement involved in this second criterion appraises and ranks desires in an order of priority made in relation to a conception of the good. The moral subject makes possible the recognition of the 'good' of the person's purpose, be it moral or prudential, and he perceives it not only as a desire to be satisfied (subjective freedom) but a desire *worth* satisfying (moral, subjective freedom). Responsibility requires that the subject self-consciously know and freely choose his purpose for the predicate 'mine' to be attached to the action.

(γ) Third, it is necessary that others recognise the action as *one's own*. This criterion holds that the intention must be validated by the other. The action must express the implicit humanity (obligation) rather than appear to be a *merely* immediate purpose and this entails that others must concur with me and my description of the good.

The protestor who stands before the division of tanks demands that others recognise the intention behind his action. Intention, therefore, requires recognition by others: 'The implementation of my end therefore has this identity of my will and the will of others within in it – it has a *positive* reference to the will of others' (§112). The first-person may be the sole judge of what is good, but his judgements are constrained by the interpretation of the other. When the Vice-president states that he did not mean to kill his friend, that it was an accident, yet we know that he owed a substantial amount of money to the victim and they were heard arguing not an hour before, then our suspicions are raised. Without the consideration of third-person expectations, first-person descriptions of actions would be our only means of evaluation and very few crimes would be punished. The agent has to be aware that his act ought to accord with the expectations of his form of life. First-person accounts of action must be intelligible to the other and this requires a standard, communal scheme of interpretation.

Action for Hegel is not simply the effect of a cause conceived of as a belief plus a desire. It is more akin to communication: I perform in order to externalise my intention and I know that the object of evaluation produced (the action) will be scrutinised and interpreted. If I wish to make myself understood, I must first be sure that we use the same language. As a language consists of rules of grammar, vocabulary and dialectical variations and also allows for novel variations, so too must an action depend upon a group of shared understandings: when I press the button on the pedestrian crossing, I want to cross the road. When I offer my hand to be grasped, I am greeting you and so on. These actions, of course rely on a shared substrate of expectations and meanings that are embodied in a culture and society.

One way to characterise this is to say that the justification of one's good or end involves one in the activity of reason-giving and this activity is, for Hegel, inherently social. There are no constraints on a will which justifies a good or a purpose to itself; one is able to convince oneself that anything may be good. Reasons for action require a degree of objectivity for Hegel and this is based on reasons being a justification for all men who share my way of life rather than just for me; that is, an actual reason rather than just wilfulness. Thus, in giving reasons, the agent knows that they are good reasons if he can convince others. It follows from this that the agent's description of his intention must harmonise with the other's interpretation of the act. A man unaware of the way in which a certain act will be interpreted, that is, how his reasons for action will be reconstructed, the tourist abroad for example, is not responsible for any offence caused although he still may be held culpable. The tourist's culpability is a legal issue arising from the consideration of what an agent ought to know on setting foot within a state. One should not expect a pork steak in Pakistan, for example. The right of objectivity not only determines who is responsible, but also who should be held responsible for ignorance. Reciprocally, the agent is only fully free when he is aware how his action will be interpreted (so the tourist is not a normal criminal, since his freedom has been compromised). The will of others contained in one's own will is this shared scheme of interpretation in and with which we describe intentions.

THE RIGHT OF OBJECTIVITY

To briefly recapitulate, Hegel's theory of action arises from a consideration of the responsible subject. He sketches what he believes are the necessary and sufficient conditions for free, moral (to use his broad term) action. It is necessary that the intention be known to the agent. People who act from neuroses or hidden motivations are not responsible for their acts. However, this is not sufficient: it could possibly be the case that a neurotic was aware of a deep trauma motivating a specific symptom, but still be unable to act otherwise. More explicitly, the coerced agent cannot be a free agent: the bank teller who hands over the money to the armed robber is not truly doing what he wants even though he is aware of his own purpose. Therefore, the subject has to freely endorse his end. Hegel puts this in terms of obligation: the intention is to be known as a good-for-me. In the case of coercion, the bank teller has a conflict of goods: self-preservation versus fulfilling his role. The former motivation trumps the latter but the agent is not free because he is not acting from his own will; it is the presence of an external factor which obstructs his free action.

Any account of action and responsibility, for Hegel, requires firstly the right of knowledge which holds that the reason on which the subject acts has to first be transcended and interrogated in terms of appropriateness: 'the fact that this moment of the *particularity* of the agent is contained and implemented in its action constitutes *subjective freedom* in its more concrete determination, i.e. the *right* of the *subject* to find its *satisfaction* in the action' (§121). Subjective, moral freedom arises from the right of knowledge (this is *my* intention) coupled with the right of intention (this is a good *for me*). It is more than the subjective freedom of the person constitutive of 'Abstract Right': the 'I want x' becomes 'I want x because it is (a) good for me'.

It would seem that these two are necessary and sufficient conditions for free action, yet Hegel adds his third determination: the intention has to be capable of reconstruction by others from the objectivity of the act itself. Hegel's originality resides in this third criterion; his theory of action retains the traditional concept of the right of knowledge of the subject, but tempers it with an objective constraint. Why is it that Hegel feels it necessary to invoke this third criterion? The answer to that question is found in the right of objectivity:

> The *right of intention* is that the *universal* quality of the action shall have being not only *in itself*, but shall be *known* by the agent and thus have been present all along in his subjective will; and conversely, what we may call the right of the *objectivity* of the action is the right of the action to assert itself as known and willed by the subject as a *thinking agent*. (§120)

The *right of intention* entails that the description of an agent's intention must be true and the agent must recognise it as such (*mens rea*). Yet, the first-person description of an intention must be constrained by the *right of objectivity of the action* whereby the interpretation of the will's intention requires a standard model of meaning; that is, a communal, inter-subjective understanding through which actions are to be recognised, categorised and judged. Without the self-certainty granted by knowledge of these categories, the subject is always unsure whether or not he has been properly recognised or if his intention can be reconstructed faithfully from his action.[2] The intention must be objective in two senses: one, it must exist outside the mind independent of the agent as a possible object of scrutiny; and two, as a description it can be true or false (§113). The right of objectivity works in two directions: first, the tourist abroad is not fully responsible until such time as he comprehends the way in which his actions are to be judged. To do this, he has to understand the expectations of others as constituted by the demands of ethical life, customs and social mores. So, it can be used in defence of the individual. Second, it can be used in prosecution of an individual: when the Vice-president claims that he has a priority in knowing what his intentions were in shooting his friend and that it was indeed an accident, this intention needs to be upheld under the scrutiny of the other. The subject may always deny what seems obvious from his action ('You've murdered him, Mr Vice-president'), but his description needs to be judged either true or false. The shared expectations, values and mores of a society are necessary for and supplement moral freedom in that they make the recognition of a subject's intention certain for both the self and the other. It is for this reason that the first two criteria on their own are not sufficient for Hegel; without the possibility of recognition, human beings cannot be fully responsible.

So, moral, subjective freedom has to be constrained by the right of objectivity. If the subject's acts are to be the expression of inwardness, then he must be certain that the other is going to reconstruct them faithfully. They must share a common understanding of the way in which acts are to be rendered intelligible. Such an understanding can only be inferred from inhabiting a shared form of life with its conception of the good and goods. The good-for-me of the subject, if valid, has to accord with the good of his social situation as interpreted via the variety of roles he occupies in his form of life. The agent knows the good in question because it is made immediately available to him through fulfilling his roles in the family (parent, child), civil society (worker) and the state (citizen). If I wish to be known as a good father, then my acts must accord with those judgements which accompany a good parent (love, generosity, discipline) and not those which are generally frowned upon (indifference, prodigality, severity).

The right of objectivity demands that the good of the particular subject and the good of the subject in the social context harmonise, otherwise the subject's acts run the risk of miscomprehension. So, the right of objectivity gives rise to objective freedom by defining those shared categories of understanding which limit and constrain the subject's projects to those that are rational, that is, can be recognised by the other. The subject's good reflects what is good for him, and it should also be recognised as a good by the other given the universal nature of good:

. . . since action is an alteration which must exist in an actual world and thus seeks recognition in it, it must in general conform to what is *recognized as valid* in that world. Whoever wills an action in the actual world has, *in so doing*, submitted himself to its laws and recognized the right of objectivity. (§132R)

Hegel, earlier in the same remark, offers an account of the relationship between *subjective* and *objective freedom* connected directly to the subjective and objective aspects of the will:

The right to recognize nothing that I do not perceive as rational is the highest right of the subject, but by virtue of its subjective determination, it is at the same time *formal*; on the other hand, *the right of the rational* – as the objective – over the subject remains firmly established.

Subjective freedom stipulates that a reason for action be recognised as valid for the agent by himself because I am not 'at home' when I act on external dictates imposed on me. The moral subject must endorse the good as his or her own good. Once more we have the celebration of the Enlightenment consciousness and this is crucial otherwise it is possible to describe the coerced or deceived (whether by state, church or other authorities) as free when it is done in their own good. It also gives us the sort of responsibility demanded by our practices of punishment:

The *right of the subjective will* is that whatever it is to recognize as valid should be *perceived* by it *as good*, and that it should be held responsible for an action – as its aim translated into external objectivity – as right or wrong, good or evil, legal or illegal, according to its cognizance of the value which that action has in this objectivity. (§132)

Abstract right was, in a very minimal sense, a form of objective freedom in that it satisfied the subjective freedom of the liberal subject's 'I want x', but the normative value of the intention's right to objectivity allows us to treat persons as subjects (and hence as criminals) because we can now fully reconstruct their intentions – as free human beings – from their actions. The satisfaction made possible by objective freedom resides in the certainty of recognition.

Whether it be the regulations of civil society which govern transactional and property law satisfying the subjective freedom of the person (I want x), to the more robust and complex institutions of the rational state which satisfy the subjective freedom of the moral subject (I want x because it is [a] good), the roles and dictates of ethical life not only determine the content of the will, but they also allow the other to recognise, categorise and judge the acts of the subject: 'And lastly, the third moment is not just the relative value of the action, but its universal value, the *good*' (§114A).

Hegel's novelty resides in the right of the objectivity of the act, which is a necessary condition for free action since it supplies the certainty of recognition required for responsibility. *Objective freedom* is the institutional and social structure of the world which makes it possible for the person or subject to satisfy his subjective freedom. It stipulates that a reason for action must accord with those categories and values of a rational form of life or ethical life. Otherwise the agent acts arbitrarily on a whim, for how can one know what is right unless one can articulate it and hold it up to the scrutiny of others? There cannot be full freedom without subjective freedom because then subjects would be mere persons: the content of their will is given by the society they happen to inhabit (think of the reason why one supports a particular football team – it is never chosen, but rather given by locale or fathers or contingent factors). This is not full freedom and any theory of action which begins from this cannot fully explain responsibility. Yet, why can we not have subjective freedom without objective freedom?

THE REJECTION OF PURELY SUBJECTIVE MORALITIES (§§129–40)

Here is a good question: what is wrong with the idea that the subject can express his intentions without relying on an immanent set of norms and values? Don't, to put it simply, actions speak for themselves? I can, after all, understand human beings from all over the globe at a basic level without the prop and support of a shared system of understandings and meanings. To expand this to the relationship between subjective and objective freedom: so long as the social structures allow me to fill my will with any content I so wish, why do I also have to have further recourse to society and culture in order to know what rational content might be? In other words, why can't we remain on the level of abstract right and propose a liberal account of the state that is concerned with the protection of basic rights and liberties and the punishment of *de facto* (rather than considering the intentions of the agent) violations.

Hegel does, in fact, have several reasons for adopting the more communitarian element of embedded values and norms, the first two being positive reasons and the final one being a negative reason: one, the notion of responsibility is incongruous in a system of punishment if one is concerned only with the *de facto* violations of rights and liberties; two, Hegel's theory of action necessitates a movement towards what he will call an 'immanent doctrine of duties' given the requirements of the right of objectivity; and three, his general rejection of subjective moralities including his famous critique of Kant is the negative reason for the appropriation of an immanent doctrine of duty. Yet, in the *Philosophy of Right*, the famous Hegelian critique of Kantian moral philosophy really only amounts to a single paragraph (§135) and he is as celebratory of Kant as he is dismissive: 'The merit and exalted viewpoint of Kant's moral philosophy are that it has emphasized the significance of duty' (§133A), and '. . . knowledge of the will first gained a firm foundation and point of departure in the philosophy of Kant' (§135A). Hegel's critique of Kant is often overstated and I sometimes wonder whether, rather than Hegel *or* Kant, one must adopt a more Hegel *and* Kant stance: Kant's account of the subjective will is able to justify its policy of action to itself through the free use of reason combined with the recognition that one's duties and values are not produced by the subjective will, but are found in the world one inhabits as Hegel suggests. That is as may be. I shall take the highly contentious step of bypassing a direct confrontation between Kant and Hegel simply because in so few pages I could not do justice to the intricacies of the Kant–Hegel debate. Such a discussion would require a proper exploration of Kant's ethical philosophy and also reference to texts of Hegel other than the *Philosophy of Right* and, to be controversial, I do not believe what is stated in the lectures we are discussing here actually requires it.[3] Hegel only needs to show that an 'immanent doctrine of duties' is necessary and he has already shown us that the concept of responsibility and his theory of action require it. But only if, of course, we can also agree that the subjective will on its own cannot tell itself what is right and good and this is why he is concerned with the rejection of subjective moralities in general. These paragraphs in the *Philosophy of Right* are meant to show that the subjective will on its own cannot determine what its duty is, and *one of* the moral philosophies that occupy such a position is Kant's. But the generality of Hegel's tone in the *Philosophy of Right* offers us an excuse to avoid some very taxing (yet very interesting – I suggest the reader follows the references) discussions in moral theory.

So, what are my duties? Hegel's answer on the surface is reactionary, but deep down it is sophisticated: we need to interrogate our way of life – with its immanent duties – to see what it says. This is at best conservatism and at worst a form of counter-Enlightenment relativism that is dangerous. For example, a contemporary moral philosopher discusses animal rights and draws an interesting parallel between the conventionally held truism of inequality between human beings and animals and certain moral problems of the past:

> Our custom is all the support that the meat industry needs. The decision to cease giving it that support may be difficult, but it is no more difficult than it would have been for a white Southerner to go against the traditions of his society and free his slaves; if we do not change our dietary habits, how can we censure those slaveholders who would not change their own way of living? (Singer, 2002, 86)

This is interesting because a slaveholder would have interrogated his way of life, the distribution of social roles and rights and liberties, and would have found philosophical, political and social support for the perpetuation of an unjust institution. What is to be celebrated in Enlightenment thought is the demand for rationality and a rationality that is to be justified to each individual and not solely to the intellectual class (the nobles, the priests, academia, etc.). Hegel did seemingly embody the Enlightenment claim that the subject must be able to see what is expected of him as a good for him (or as right) and, if all that means is referring to the values and norms of one's culture, then the right of subjectivity seems a vacuous operation. Hegel's discussion of abstract right has already, as we have seen in the last chapter, committed him to the norm of equality once a specific historical structure is in place; and this rules out the institution of slavery because:

> When the existing world of freedom has become unfaithful to the better will, this will no longer finds itself in the duties recognized

in this world and must seek to recover in ideal inwardness alone that harmony which it has lost in actuality. (§138R)

Hegel is aware that the customs, mores and values of a society may not be 'rational' and, as such, the moral will cannot be at home in them. And this unhomeliness can articulate itself as a demand for change. In such a society, radical critique is possible but it is as likely to make things worse as it is to make things better due to its arbitrariness.[4] Such a demand on the part of individual reason for change is the very spirit of the Enlightenment. Enlightenment moral philosophy is, of course, best exemplified in Kant's claim that it is the individual and his or her own reason, not the dictates of state, which determine what his or her duty is (Kant, 1991, 54 and 59; Kant, 1993, Aix, fn.). So, what exactly is Hegel up to?

Well, the subject cannot decide what is right or good contingently, otherwise we have a form of subjectivism and that will, on the one hand, undermine the structures of our understanding of others' actions (imagine if everyone could use their own words and rules of grammar) and, on the other, there would be no objective way to say that is right and that is wrong only that is right-for-me or wrong-for-me. Of course, Kant agrees and he tries to show that duties can be derived from a prior principle that meets the requirements of rationality, viz. the categorical imperative. Other less sophisticated writers may tell us that the voice of conscience will speak to us and naturally guide us. Let us look at Hegel's discussion of all of these positions without trying to delve too deeply into very large historical disputes. The main upshot of Hegel's criticism of these attempts to ground right and wrong in the individual is that such positions are unable to resolve conflicts and tell us exactly what our duties are. Resolution requires an objective set of duties properly ordered and such a set will be found through the interrogation of one's roles and place in society (by making an appeal to a set of norms and values we all share, viz. *Sittlichkeit*), and these will be ultimately justified by their historical development.

Hegel in his discussion of 'The Good and Conscience' has a particular ethical enemy in sight. When he earlier describes the first-person point of view as 'inviolable' he was ever ready to temper his assertion with the right of objectivity of the intention. Why? Well, for one, we will never be able to detect cases of deception: 'You say I did X, but I didn't mean to.' Second, Hegel has in mind a more pertinent moral position. The worth of a moral act is whether or not the agent intended to do what is right, but how does the agent know what is right? This is the same as asking: how does the agent know what his duty is? If the subjective will can determine what its duties are, then there is no need for an immanent doctrine of duties and Hegel's social ethics is undone before it starts. So, how would it be possible for the subjective will to know what is good on its own and without recourse to external considerations? Hegel deals explicitly with three possible answers to this question:

i)   the will knows immediately what its duty is;
ii) duties can be derived from some prior principle of reason (Kant proper, let us say); and
iii) the individual need only listen to the voice of his or her conscience to tell him or her what is good.

Immediate knowledge of right and wrong, good and evil

The trouble with the claim that the subjective will knows immediately what is good is that it cannot explain why there are conflicts between the right and welfare. I know what it is right to do and I know what is good for me and others. However, sometimes these will come into conflict and I am unable to decide between them by appealing to what I know to be good. One moral law is 'Do not steal' and we know this to be a duty. But surely another duty is to cultivate oneself, to persevere, and these two duties may come into conflict when I find myself destitute and without the possibility to legitimately acquire sustenance, as Raskolnikov does in *Crime and Punishment*. In this conflict how do we know which is the duty? Remember that conflicts arise between rights, but they now arise between welfare and rights; it is good for me to preserve my life, but I am poor and can only do so if I steal:

> The *particularity* of the interests of the natural will, taken together as a simple *totality*, is personal existence as *life*. *In extreme danger* and in collision with the rightful property of someone else, this life may claim (not in equity, but as a right) a *right of necessity*, for the alternatives are an infinite injury to existence with total loss of rights, and an injury only to an individual and limited existence of freedom, whereby right as such

and the capacity for rights of the injured party, who has been injured only in *this* specific property, continue to be recognized. (§127)

And the addition makes Hegel's exact meaning much clearer: 'Life, as the totality of ends, has a right in opposition to abstract right . . . If someone whose life is in danger were not allowed to take measures to save himself, he would be destined to forfeit all his rights; and since he would be deprived of life, his entire freedom would be negated.' Hegel is once again playing on common-sense concerns: should I let myself die in order to be dutiful to the law not to steal? Most of us would agree that any morality which advocated this would be too demanding.

The collision between the right and the good understood as that which is to be maximised by teleological ethics (welfare, happiness, etc.) has in fact become the defining debate of modern ethics.[5] We acknowledge that people's welfare is a good, and we also acknowledge that it is wrong to punish the innocent. But what if our only way to make a terrorist tell us the whereabouts of his bomb that would kill a thousand people is by torturing his young sister before his eyes? Should we consider the welfare of people more important than the punishing of the innocent? Can any appeal to the subjective will or conscience resolve such conflicts?

As persons we claim and recognise rights. As moral subjects, we claim responsibility for our actions and pursue what we consider to be good broadly conceived. What I see as good is not necessarily what is right and there will be instances of conflict that seem irresolvable. And the irresolvable nature of these conflicts is a puzzle to the will because the notion of good is universal and the claims of right and welfare which pull immediately on my practical reason ought to harmonise, if there is to be a truly moral way to act (§129). Reasons for action come from desires, beliefs, notions of right, considerations of welfare, and if there is to be an answer to 'What should I do?', then these cannot come into conflict. Good becomes explicitly moral good and this is universal, in the sense of free of the agent: '[The subjective will] thus stands in a relationship to the good, a relationship whereby the good *ought* to be its substantial character, whereby it ought to make the good its end and fulfil it' (§131).

How do we resolve conflicts between welfare and right? The question becomes explicitly moral – in the sense we now inhabit the terrain we like to think of as moral philosophy proper – and the subject is forced to ask him or herself: what *ought* I to do? The claim that the subjective will has an immediate answer to this question is simply vain and false:

> Since action for itself requires a particular content and a deter-
> minate end, whereas duty in the abstract contains nothing of the
> kind, the question arises: *what is duty?* For this definition, all that
> is available so far is this: to do *right*, and to promote *welfare*, one's
> own welfare and welfare in its universal determination, the
> welfare of others. (§134)

When the subject asks himself as an individual what his duty is, he can find only two: the formal nature of equality and right derived from his own abstract rights that entail the recognition of others' rights, and the idea of good as the satisfaction and achievement of his desires, preferences and projects. The satisfaction of these also has a universal element: just as my rights entail the rights of others, so my welfare entails that the welfare of others has a value. When I act towards a goal it is important for me to achieve that goal, and so it has a value for me. I demand a right to achieve it as a person, so it must also have formal value for you. But the substantial goal of my action may not have value for you, neither does the fact that I achieve the goal and not someone else. So, if my action embodies a reason to pursue a goal then this has value because the pursuit of goals and their achievement is a value. But I can only make such a claim if you recognise this to be the case and this means that the achievement of goals is in some sense a value for all (§119). However, to say that the more people who achieve their goals and projects the better does not prescribe any specific duties. It is tantamount to the prescriptions: 'Do right, promote welfare.' The question is: how?

The subjective will cannot overcome conflicts of duty. The sub-
jective will unconstrained by the right of objectivity will generate contradictions with two main origins: first, contradictions between self-interest and other duties (my particular well-being versus the rights of other persons, and more concretely the duties of my social roles); but also conflicts between the many kinds of duties (the family versus the state, for example). To say that duty trumps self-interest is a possible response to the former dilemma, but not to the second, and Hegel would not endorse it even for the former conflict

(remember the case when one is starving and can only acquire food through theft; here we have a case of the right of necessity). Freedom is self-determination, but if duty contradicts happiness can I truly be said to be acting from my own will if it is true that I still want what I did not do?

Duties can be derived from some prior principle of reason

Some moral thinkers (like Kant) believe that this question can be answered through the dictates of reason, through self-reflection or through a special moral faculty. In other words, the subject himself can divine what his or her duties are. We know what sorts of motives or reasons for actions are wrong and which are required because we are able to either test (weak version) or generate (strong version) them from a more fundamental principle of practical reason, viz. the categorical imperative. Moral obligations come from reason. Kant's account is obviously in Hegel's sights and it would be worthwhile to offer the barest features of that account before moving on.[6]

I should stress before I begin that this brief account of Kant's ethics will not do justice to his work. For Hegel, the common-sense idea that an agent is motivated to act in a certain way because he finds satisfaction in achieving his end is not problematic as it was for Kant. To badly caricature, Kant's moral philosophy originates from the idea of the good will which we can characterise as doing the right thing for the right reasons. So, if we know breaking a promise is wrong, then the man who breaks a promise (does the wrong thing) cannot be redeemed by his motive (to protect someone, he has reneged on a promise to supply information to an unjust persecuting authority). Neither can one do the right thing for the wrong reasons, such as personal gain, like the shopkeeper who charges fair prices only because it increases his custom. Yet, this raises an epistemological problem: how do we know when someone has acted on the good will? Kant's answer is robust: we are sure when an agent acts morally when his inclinations contradict his duty and yet he still performs his duty:

> For, in the case of what is to be morally good it is not enough that it *conform* with the moral law but it must also be done *for the sake of the law*; without this, that conformity is only very contingent and precarious, since a ground that is not moral will indeed now

and then produce actions in conformity with the law, but it will also often produce actions contrary to the law. (Kant, 1997, 3–4)

The Kantian moral will must be motivated by practical reason and not empirical causes. Let us think about this a little more deeply. An agent may perform an act *from duty*: you do it because you believe it is the right thing to do; or *from immediate inclination*: you like doing it (the person who volunteers to work in a charity shop because he enjoys helping people); or because *impelled through another inclination*: the action is a necessary means to achieve some other end (the merchant who prices his goods fairly because otherwise he will lose custom and it will affect his wealth). This gives us a taxonomy of motives when reasons for action and inclinations are in place:

(a) one does one's duty in spite of inclination (if I break my promise I'll benefit massively, but it is the wrong thing to do);
(b) one does one's duty in accordance with one's inclination (it is right to help people, and I enjoy doing it);
(c) one acts on inclination but is in accordance with duty (I love helping people, so I volunteer every Saturday to work in the Oxfam shop);
(d) one acts on inclination contrary to duty (I break my promise for personal benefit).

Now (a) is Kant's paradigmatic account of moral worth because we are sure that in this case an agent acts on moral duty. The trouble with (c) is that we very often mix it up with (b) and vice versa, it is an epistemic and not an ethical problem. So, one possibility is that Kant is going to concentrate on (a) because it is the most obvious case, but Hegel understands Kant as saying something stronger: only when the subject acts from duty alone does an action have any moral worth.

For Kant, what counts with moral deeds is not the action one sees, but the principle on which one acted and only those principles characteristic of a good will are morally praiseworthy. The good will is the embodiment of autonomy for Kant because man's capacity to represent laws to himself offers him the freedom to act in accordance with or contrary to them: once I know what is right, I ought to obey. A law is an objective representation of a maxim and when a subjective principle of action can be formulated as a law, it then becomes a practical necessity to act upon it. Human beings act both in accordance with laws (as objects do); but also in accordance with their representation of laws (as objects do not). This opens a gap between our subjective principles (how we actually do act) and objective laws of practical reason (how we ought to act) and, on one reading of Kant, actions are morally praiseworthy when I act on the dictates of reason and not on the compulsion of other motivations (desires, preferences, emotions). I am autonomous and free when I legislate myself.

As such, the laws of reason will have practical necessity and this can be understood via a comparison with logical necessity: if I believe that all triangles have three sides and the shape before my eyes has four sides, it is illogical for me to believe it is a triangle. One can be mistaken about one's beliefs, but if one held both of these beliefs, then it would be impossible at the cost of rationality to assert that the shape before me is a triangle. The impossibility is grounded in a law of reasoning for Kant: one cannot form judgements unless one obeys certain logical principles. One cannot think in any other way because that would not constitute thinking. Logical necessity holds that if a is b and b is c, then a is c; rational necessity holds that if you believe that a is b and you believe that b is c, then you must believe that a is c.

The necessity in moral obligation is rational necessity: it concerns what you must do given certain judgements. Kant wants to show that practical judgements have a similar necessity: if you believe that x is right, then you must – at the cost of rationality – do x no matter what you want, need or feel (all of these factors are, after all, contingent). But how do we know what is right? Kant needs to show that the moral law is a principle of practical reason. Well, we know when a mere motivation or consideration for action becomes a law because it fits the model of the categorical imperative: by universalising our motive, we see whether this is or is not a law: 'act only in accordance with that maxim through which you can at the same time will that it become a universal law' (Kant, 1997, 31).[7] A problematically simple way of understanding the use of the categorical imperative is that a principle of action must hold always, everywhere and for everyone in order to qualify as a law as opposed to a mere motivation. This rules out any reference to desires or preferences since these will always be agent relative. If the motivation contains a contradiction when universalised, then the action is forbidden and its opposite is required. If the motivation can be universalised without contradiction, then the action is permissible. If an agent is rational, then he or she is governed by the categorical imperative in all matters.

How are we to understand the claim that an intention that contains a contradiction when universalised is forbidden? In the text, Kant distinguishes between two types of contradiction (Kant, 1997, 33): first, the contradiction in conception test – your maxim cannot be thought of as a universal law without contradiction (I assert x and not x at the same time) which is, of course, impossible at the cost of reason to assert. Take, for example, the maxim 'I want to be a slaveholder' (O'Neill, 1989, 96). There is nothing contradictory in an individual wanting to become a slaveholder, but the moral worthiness of my actions concerns their universal element, that is when the maxim applies to all men, at all times and in all places. And it is here that the contradiction arises when I make the maxim universal: 'Everyone ought to be slaveholder.' If everyone willed to be a slaveholder, then everybody would hold some property and there would be no one without property and, hence, no slaves. Without slaves, there can be no slaveholders. The universal maxim is inconceivable according to Kant because in asserting the obligation one knows what duty demands but acts in violation of it: I can only will that I become a slaveholder when I simultaneously will that others do not and, as such, I make myself a special case and an exception to the law.

Secondly, certain laws are not contradictory if conceived, but do become contradictory when put into practice, so there is also the contradiction in will test – your maxim can be thought of as a universal law, but not willed as a universal law without contradiction: I can conceive of the course of action (x), but I cannot will x since it involves willing x and not x at the same time. Take the example of refusing to accept help when I require it (O'Neill, 1989, 100). As an individual, it is not contradictory to refuse help when it is required and even when the maxim's universal element is brought out (everyone ought to refuse help when they require it), there is no contradiction of the logical sort detailed above (it is logically possible to have a world like this but logically impossible to have a world with slaveholders but no slaves). The universal principle that everyone ought to refuse help when they require it is not logically impossible but it does violate the principle of hypothetical reason: if I will an end I must be committed to willing the means to that end. If one commits all persons to refusing help when required, one is committing all persons to sometimes will an end but not will the means to that end (there will be times when, in order to achieve my goal, I will require the help of others) and this is irrational.

Hegel firstly sees a problem with the Kantian picture involving motivation: if reason has to be divorced from self-interest or desires and drives in general, as Kant assumes it must for the agent to act freely, then practical reason must be the source of duty. Kant would agree: the good will cannot be an inclination or a given desire of man for attaining satisfaction since the free play of reason would become superfluous. One would be 'coaxed' (natural necessity) into being good and moral actions would lose their worth – they need to be spontaneous in the same way judgements are spontaneous for Kant. And since reason will say the same thing to all men, it is universal and impartial, then a duty will not be my duty, but all men's duty. Kant would once more agree. But, if the 'my' in the sense of seeing it as a 'good' disappears from the table, then why should I be moral? (§133). Why should I do my duty? Kant's answer, according to Hegel, is that one ought to do one's duty because it is one's duty, or duty for duty's sake. This reading is supported by Kant's language, but it is highly problematic and controversial since the claim that only acting for the sake of a moral law is morally praiseworthy just does not agree with our moral intuitions. Sympathy, we might want to hold, is praiseworthy and cruelty is blameworthy. And this is Hegel's point: although I am not motivated by the satisfaction I attain by doing a right act, the fact that I am satisfied by so doing it is just part of human nature. To separate reason and desire in this forced way is to misunderstand human psychology and promote a morality of 'duty for duty's sake' (§135R). Moral action is, to return to a theme, concerned with purifying desires not transcending them.

Kant would perhaps have responded that duty is practically necessary and does not require any empirical motivation. Yet, such a response opens him up to Hegel's further challenges. Practical reason is unable to dictate what we ought to do without considering what we want, or what we happen to consider of value because, according to Hegel, duty for duty's sake is either an empty formalism, or it is too strict and demands too much of the particular moral agent. The belief that the rationality of the subjective will can supply determinations for the will from pure reason is simply misguided because it is too abstract. These considerations constitute the empty formalism charge: the categorical imperative tells us the form of a moral imperative, that it must have the form of a universal law, but can tell us nothing about its content/material: 'The criterion of law which Reason possesses within itself fits every case equally well, and is thus in fact no criterion at all' (PhG, ¶431). Hegel's claim is that the content of moral laws must be drawn from the actual social world one inhabits. If you tell me to respect the dead, and I agree, we may still disagree about how: the Greeks tell me to burn my dead and the Callatians tell me to eat them (Herodotus, 1936, 160–1). The form of the law tells us about its rightness, but it cannot give us an account of what we should do since that requires a system of meanings, values and goods. Hegel's favourite example is the institution of private property: theft is wrong because one both recognises the institution of private property and violates it in stealing and, as such, you undermine the institution you assert. One cannot universalise a principle of action such as 'I shall take what is not mine when my interests require it'. Yet, such a law is not unconditional because it relies on the fact that individuals recognise the institution of private property which is dependent on particular social structures and contingencies (§135R). One could imagine principles of property distribution ('the nobles deserve what they are able to appropriate with force') that would agree with the above principle but still condone acts we would consider to be theft.

Yet, the criticism of empty formalism may be misguided. Kant may say that the categorical imperative can generate duties: do not lie, do not break promises, which are perfect and required. But, in this case, the universal law is too strict. On the one hand, we are left once more in the grip of conflicts of duties: should I not break my promise even if it can save a life? And on the other hand, the demands to 'help the poor' or 'love one's enemies' are ones which the categorical imperative shows to be forbidden. If we universalise them, we have a contradiction because in helping the poor I stop them being poor and hence in a universalised world, the contradiction would arise because I would annihilate that very thing I was trying to help (NL, 127). So we ought not help the poor nor love our enemies, according to the demands of the categorical imperative.

Alternatively, it is possible that Kant never intended the categorical imperative to generate principles of action, but only to test them. Thus, the moral agent can derive his or her obligations from the social fabric, but he or she ought to rationally interrogate them and that would amount to testing them by the categorical imperative to see if they are in fact valid. What if the categorical imperative were merely a way to test duties? If they do not contain a contradiction when willed, if they can have the form of universal law, if they do not make the agent an exception and if they could be willed as a law in a possible kingdom of ends, then it is required of the agent. Hegel says fine, but the determinations of the will (the duties) cannot just be magicked up, they have to be given to the will. The subject is unable to generate determinations of the will out of his reflective understanding, as its abstractness needs to be overcome by objective determinations; that is, the individual can only be free in an objective, moral order which expresses his intelligibility and informs his intentions as to the way in which their external nature will be comprehended by others; that is, in a moral fabric which makes the satisfaction of his rational desires and aspirations possible. Universal values such as respect, sympathy, goodness are available for the subject but how one is able to express them is relative to the substantial moral fabric which one inhabits. Shaking someone's hand might be a sign of respect, but it could just as equally be an action which causes great offence. Hegel's point is simply that the nature of universal moral imperatives which are derived from reason is not that they are wrong, but simply that they need to be substantial and substance comes from social practices. The content of these social practices is not a matter of philosophical concern, but is to be found embedded and present in our culture. And, if this is the case, then Kant's moral psychology is wrong since it is not duty for duty's sake that motivates the agent.

The conscience

Hegel's rejection of the conscience as a mode for determining one's duties is rather simple. The conscience is arbitrary and cannot provide a ground for objective judgements concerning right and wrong, good and evil. The moral point of view has to be constrained because it is infinitely powerful and can posit (or negate) any good whatsoever as universal good: '. . . conscience know itself as thought, and that this thought of mine is my sole source of obligation' (§136A); and '*Conscience* expresses the absolute entitlement of subjective self-consciousness to know *in itself* and *from itself* what rights and duty are, and to recognize only what it thus knows as the good; it also consists in the assertion that what it thus knows and wills is *truly* right and duty' (§137R). Due to the abstract nature of the good, the conscience can endorse any content subjectively. Pathological examples of this phenomenon include asceticism, the Terror of revolutions and the stance of irony:

> Although it has a relation to this objectivity, it at the same time distances itself from it and knows itself as that which wills and resolves in a particular way but may equally well will and resolve otherwise. – 'You in fact honestly accept a law as existing in and for itself' [it says to others]; 'I do so, too, but I go further than you, for I am also beyond this law and can do this or that as I please. It is not the thing which is excellent, it is I who am excellent and master of both law and thing; I merely play with them as with my own caprice, and in this ironic consciousness in which I let the highest of things perish, I merely enjoy myself.' (§140R)

The ironic stance negates the objectivity of value in favour of its own individual power, that of the subjective will of the agent: '. . . it is no longer someone else's authority or assertion that counts, but the subject itself, i.e. its own conviction, which can alone make something good' (§140R). Here it is only necessary to remind the reader that, for Hegel, reason-giving is a social and not a theoretical activity, certainty can only be granted to the subject from another subject not from himself.

More importantly, Hegel sees the appeal to an individual conscience as contradictory: 'The conscience is therefore subject to judgment as to its *truth* or falsity, and its appeal solely to *itself* is directly opposed to what it seeks to be – that is, the rule for a rational and universal mode of action which is valid in and for itself' (§137R). The thinker who appeals to conscience wants to hold that moral statements can be true or false, yet how do we know whether they are true or false? The appeal is made to the individual and his conscience and there exists no other standard of truth.

TRANSITION TO ETHICAL LIFE

The significance of the dismissal of the simple approach of modern normative ethics that seeks to prescribe what ought to be is to move away from an approach which either lists moral laws or shows how moral laws can be considered right through consistency with a prior principle. Instead, Hegel wants to show that the normative commitments of one's social and moral fabric can be the only guide to action. The advantage of Hegel's approach is best exemplified through the use of one of the most commonly invoked moral dilemmas: the mother who has to decide whether or not to steal to feed her starving child. It is good to feed the child, but it is wrong to steal. The universality of good means that these two goods should harmonise, yet the moral conscience is quite able to accept one as right at the expense of the other in one moment, then – in the next second – to reverse such a description. For Hegel, the moral conscience itself cannot decide between conflicting determinations of the will and, if it does so, such a decision is wholly arbitrary.

The solution, for Hegel, is firstly to make an appeal to the norms and values of society, but even here the conflict does not dissipate. The immediate determination of the family, the naturally binding duty of the maternal bond, gives rise to the desire to protect, feed and sustain the child. This is the good-for-mother. Yet, her role in civil society determines that she recognise the rationality of the right to property and this, too, is a good. So, how would Hegel articulate this conflict? The answer is to return to the idea that 'the existing world of freedom has become unfaithful to the better will' when 'this will no longer finds itself in the duties recognized in this world'. The mother is not at home in such a world because the demands she faces cannot be answered by the normative structures of will before her. So, a new demand has to be made on ethical life itself: what gives rise to the conflict? That a child be fed is a good and that the right of property be respected is a good, so such a society in which a conflict between these two is felt is *not* rational because the mother cannot act freely. She is torn, divided and not at home within her culture. The conflict can only be overcome when objective freedom, granted by the institutions of ethical life, eradicates the existence of the mother's need to steal and her subjective freedom can be satisfied (through the supply of basic needs as a right (the welfare state) and the eradication of poverty, or legal recognition of her subjective freedom adjudicated in a court).

Hegel realises that the abstract nature of the good cannot be created from the top down and theoretically tested. It is not truly possible for the agent to declare what the world ought to be like in all certainty given the dictates of reason. Instead, the moral subject must begin from the existing world and its institutions since the constraint of objectivity involves the idea that the good must be intelligible to these institutions (§141). Only in such a way can subjective freedom meet the constraint of objective freedom and, reciprocally, it is this very objective freedom which grants the subject the certainty of recognition he requires to satisfy his actions. Therefore, it is only the ethical subject who is truly free:

> The ethical person is conscious of the content of his action as something necessary, something that is valid in and for itself, and this consciousness is so far from diminishing freedom, that, on the contrary, it is only through this consciousness that his abstract freedom becomes a freedom that is actual and rich in content, as distinct from freedom of choice [*Willkür*], a freedom that still lacks content and is merely possible. (EL, §158A)

The mother is faced with an arbitrary choice to make, yet in a rational society she would be offered a rational choice, one that is resolvable. The objective freedom of ethical life makes possible the satisfaction of rational desires, projects and aspirations and the three institutions of modern society – that is, the family, civil society and the modern political state – all combine to fulfil these conditions of objective freedom. It is these determinations of ethical life which constitute the objective freedom of the subject in that they enable him to satisfy his desires, wants and aspirations, to simultaneously pursue the good, and to be certain of recognition by the other. Hegel's claim, then, is that the subject as he has described it in 'Morality' can only be fully free when his or her objective freedom is secured by these modern institutions.

Study Questions

1. What role does the concept of responsibility play in Hegel's theory of action?
2. Appraise Hegel's critique of Kant. Is Kantian morality to be wholly rejected or does it have a place in discussions of modern subjectivity?

CHAPTER 7

ETHICAL LIFE: SOCIAL FREEDOM

PREAMBLE

Hegel's introduction was predominantly concerned with the comprehension of metaphysical freedom, abstract right with personal freedom, morality with moral freedom and the last part of his lecture series is concerned with the missing part of the jigsaw: social freedom. How free am I in this society? Do its laws and customs oppress or liberate me? Why should I obey them?

When social and political structures are rational, according to Hegel, they maintain and promote the objective freedom of abstract right, the subjective freedom of morality and also allow the individual the freedom to express his or her rational existence. Abstract right protects the individual's pursuit of his or her interests, morality explains how we feel at home in a society which allows us to be responsible for our own interests and ethical life is going to tell us which interests are rational, that is the ones we ought to pursue. Ethical life will confer on our interests a standard of objectivity. From the discussion of morality, we have learned that Hegel rejects our normal normative understanding of ethics or the 'ought to be' which regulates what we should do in terms of general prior principles. Hegel's alternative is *Sittlichkeit* or ethical life constituted by the mores, customs and laws of a society, and these are a form of freedom because they liberate the individual from erroneous or purely subjective motivations for action. *Sittlichkeit* describes how a subject can know his or her duties because social existence constitutes and determines right behaviour and these duties will be *rational* when they are actual and not merely existent:

Ethical life is the *Idea of freedom* as the living good which has its knowledge and volition in self-consciousness, and its actuality through self-conscious action. Similarly, it is an ethical being that self-consciousness has its motivating end and a foundation which has being in and for itself. Ethical life is accordingly the *concept of freedom which has become the existing world and the nature of self-consciousness.* (§142)

I act freely when I am certain I act rationally and I act rationally when my values are true. Such certainty requires the rational state and not just any state, one whose structures and roles are those that I would endorse as a free individual. The rational state requires the subjective will of the individual, but also needs to supply the objective freedom whereby the self-conscious subject knows what is right and freely endorses it.

Ethical life, in other words, incorporates the subjective and objective elements of freedom in the actualisation of those categories, values and meanings which make human freedom possible. The agent is free when he or she pursues what is good (objective freedom) conscious of it being good (subjective freedom). It is important that we do not fall into an error about the standard of objectivity of ethical life which could be understood in two ways. On the one hand, any ethical life will allow the subject to order, prioritise and purify desire, and hence supply the subject with a standard of objectivity. This is the theory of value relativism: a moral judgement is true if it coheres with the judgement of a specific culture. We could say, then, that subjects are free if the objective, institutional order coupled with the subjective knowledge of these determinations constrain the actions of the subject within the bounds of intelligibility given *whichever* form of life; or just because humans *happen* to exist in communities. So, the victim who consents to be ritually sacrificed is free when she knows the reason why she must be sacrificed (for a good harvest) and such a reason is coherent with the order of a specific society. But, such purification will not be rational in Hegel's view and there would be something seriously amiss if that were all subjective freedom amounted to. Ethical life is not merely a form of life which determines and harmonises the good; *rather* it is the rational order. The Hegelian position holds that objective freedom satisfies the requirements of the subjective will but he has to demonstrate – in order to avoid the charge of relativism – that the structures and categories he proposes are the necessary end of the development of human society.

THE CONCEPT OF ETHICAL LIFE (§§142–157)

Ethical life, ways of life and the social thesis

It is possible that you support a football team and, if not, it is not so hard to imagine what being a supporter of a football team may involve. If you were to ask yourself why you support a specific team, say Aston Villa, there may well be a story to tell: they were the local team, they won the European Cup when you were a child or, oddly, you liked the colour of their kit. However, none of these stories *justify* your supporting this team; it is a just a fact of your existence that you were thrown into the role of being an Aston Villa supporter (for better or worse). Yet, if one were to be rational about this, to be a man of the Enlightenment and seek criteria for the support of a specific team (history, success, association with legendary players, and so on), it would be possible to stand back and apply these 'transcendental' reasons to choose the team who 'score' the most points. But such a reasoner would not be a real supporter, not in the sense in which we use the word, or at best they would be a Manchester United fan. The idea that there exists an original position of rationality to choose one's own essential, social character is a chimera. One is thrown into a community with its values, meanings and reasons produced from a long tradition and history. One just is social and this social nature determines how one behaves. This is the nature of Hegel's novel concept of ethical life.[1]

If I were to characterise what ethical life is, I would probably say that it incorporates those values and norms which govern the subject's practical reasoning and pre-exist him, deriving from his role in and his being a member of a certain society:

> The fact that the ethical sphere is the *system* of these determinations of the Idea constitutes its *rationality*. In this way, the ethical sphere is freedom, or the will which has being in and for itself as objectivity, as a circle of necessity whose moments are the *ethical powers* which govern the lives of individuals. (§145)[2]

So, as an Aston Villa supporter it makes sense to watch the football results on Saturday and wear claret and blue when I play football when it would not for another supporter or person. The communitarian aspect of Hegel's thought is most clearly revealed in the claim that since the human is a child of his time, he or she has a relationship to the state that is closer than trust (§147). The subject as a member of the rational order has an identity which motivates him in certain situations: 'Thus, without any selective reflection, the person performs his duty *as his own* and as something which *is*; and in this necessity *he* has himself and his actual freedom' (EG, §514). The member of *Sittlichkeit* can perform his or her duties – possibly from habit, that is without any 'selective reflection' – because they constitute his identity. It is not how he *should* act, it is how he *does* act (I cheer when Aston Villa score because I am a fan; I drive on the left because I am English), and he can be certain of recognition as an agent through fulfilling the dictates of these roles. Ethical substance is constructed from objective laws, customs and mores – that is both formal and substantive modes of behaviour – which are reciprocally felt as subjective duties: I care because I am the father, I generate wealth because I am a unit of the market, I cheer the goal because I am an Aston Villa fan (notice how being an *abstract* football fan cannot generate behaviour or expectations of behaviour!) and so on:

> All these substantial determinations are *duties* which are binding on the will of the individual; for the individual, as subjective and inherently undetermined – or determined in a particular way – is distinct from them and *consequently stands in a relationship to them* as to his own substantial being. (§148)

It is both the objective social order embedded in institutions and also the substantial identity of the agent as a member of these institutions. *Sittlichkeit* constitutes one's identity by defining me as part of a whole and prescribing those duties and obligations I must fulfil and those values I must exhibit as a part of this whole. I act according to those norms and values which are embedded in the moral fabric of my society and I ensure that these norms and values are enforced through my adherence to them. Thus, the rational state and its structure constitute the objective freedom of the individual.

Sittlichkeit is, in many ways, Hegel's most distinctive ethical theory and concurs with the social thesis of contemporary political philosophy.[3] The social thesis can be descriptively characterised as the claim that the individual subject is only who he (or she) is by virtue of the society and tradition which brought him into being and which maintains and promotes his identity. The values he holds dear, which justify political institutions and arrangements and which play a role in the subject's practical reasoning, are themselves products of, rather than the basis for, his community. However, it is easy to see how such a view is susceptible to the charge of relativism: the slave-holder may be constituted by a society that incorporates a principle of natural inequality or divine providence. The social thesis, if it is not a mere sociological truism, has to demonstrate *how* and *why* certain societies with their inherent meanings, values and norms are better than others. So, normatively, the adherent of the social thesis has to hold that a specific society (or law, etc.) is better (that is, more desirable, rational, worthwhile) than others and justify this claim. Such justification cannot, as we have seen with the football fan, be transcendental but must be immanent. The social world is the world of actualised freedom and its institutions either inhibit or promote freedom. Human freedom can be obstructed under certain condi-tions, but we cannot rationally and *a priori* predict what these insti-tutions are or which ones will be rational. Just as the works of our literary canon can be described as the best that has been written and said, it is not possible to derive criteria from its members that need to be met in order for a work of literature to be included in the set. The understanding attempts this, but comprehension is aware that the human is a child of his time. Human beings are bound by history and must let history decide, slowly sorting rational wheat from contingent chaff. But just as we cannot say now who will enter the literary canon in the future, we cannot – it seems – be certain of our values and norms unless there is a further justification of their rationality.

The rationality of *Sittlichkeit*

The challenge faced by all adherents of the social thesis and, there-fore, also Hegel is the question how I am able to know that the laws, institutions of my society are rational, if they constitute my essence and, hence, my standard of rationality. Liberalism, with its transcen-dental approach, can offer us a critical perspective since the values of liberty and equality transcend society, but Hegel rejects such an approach. *Sittlichkeit* is, as we have seen, the world constructed by social reasons for actions. It supplies motivations and obligations for the agent in virtue of his membership and his role in this institutional order. When a man I meet on the street offers me his hand, his action does not *cause* me to shake his hand, it is *meaningful*. My response, in taking his hand, is a habit arising from the behavioural norms of my society and its institutions. It could so well be different and *mean* something else in a different social context. The social mores and customs of my community allow me to understand the intentions of others through their actions and they also determine the appropriate responses to such behaviour. In this sense, *Sittlichkeit* is a 'second nature', the world is constituted by social rather than natural reasons for action (§151). These reasons remain reflective even if they are not reflected upon. This difference is probably best illustrated by Hegel's own distinction between reflective (the state) and unreflective trust (the family). The difference lies in the possibility of articulating and therefore sharing one's reasons for action. If I am to save my child from drowning or, on a lesser scale, to provide for the material needs of my family, I cannot truly articulate the reason why I fulfil this role. The best I can manage is 'Because they are my family'. Moreover, someone who demands that I justify my reasons for these actions is simply inhuman, not in the sense of evil, but in the sense that they cannot truly comprehend what it is to be a human being. These reasons, then, are immediate and unreflective, and trust in one's family members is based on the same disposition. The reflective trust in the state, however, is open to scrutiny. It is perfectly sensible to demand a justification of a particular law, social duty or more, and why I should act in accordance with it; although in stable states this need is felt less and citizens trust more.

But what does this scrutiny amount to if the standard that the society must meet is articulated in terms of values derived from that society? You tell me it is not rational to support Aston Villa, but I tell you that – from within the community of Aston Villa supporters – nothing could be more rational. To avoid the charge of relativism, Hegel must make his immanent critique bite and his account of social freedom allows us to articulate two norms that constitute the rational state as opposed to any particular state: one, laws and institutions of the rational state have to secure the basic material needs of the members so that agents are not bound by their immediate desires (they are free from dependence and have a sphere of personal choice); and two, it must be possible for agents to endorse

the laws of the rational state and recognise their underlying rationality such that it is something which they would freely do (that is,
feel at home in them) (Neuhouser, 2000, chap. 4). Both of these
claims are immanent in Hegel's historico-philosophical comprehension of the concept of freedom.

First, ethical life is the substantial description of the possible
determinations of one of its members and is, then, liberation and
freedom because it purifies and rationalises the drives of the individual (§19). Duty for Hegel is liberation and not a limitation; it
appears as a limitation only in the spheres of abstract right (the
natural will) and morality. Objective freedom is freedom because it
liberates the subject in three ways:

a) from a dependence on immediate drives;
b) from partiality to itself (egoism), which is necessary for firm
   social relationships to be set up that augment the individuals'
   freedom (cooperation);
c) from having to produce the categories for comprehension
   (values, rights and duties) for himself *ex nihilo* and from the need
   to determine good from his own conscience (§149).

Hegel's first normative claim is that certain societies are more rational than others because a rational moral fabric must objectively
protect the rights of autonomous individuals, those rights first outlined in 'Abstract Right'. Since the will is free, laws and conventions
ought to be expressions of freedom (either through allowing a
rational choice or enforcing the realm of subjective freedom). An
irrational law, institution or more obstructs the subjective freedom
of rational choice (§144). Hegel transforms the Kantian 'man as
end' into a political statement by reformulating it as the demand
that man must be recognised as a rational subject and, as such, he
commands rights: 'My will is a rational will; it has validity, and this
validity should be recognised by others' (217A).[4] Thus, my will is a
particular will because it expresses what is rational: 'The right of
individuals to their *particularity* is likewise contained in ethical
substantiality, for particularity is the mode of outward appearance
in which the ethical exists' (§154). So, normatively in the rational
state, slavery is outlawed (§137), practices of religions are constrained by personal rights (implicitly asserting the modern division of state and church) (§270R) and careers are open to talent
(§§206, 277).

Secondly, certain societies are more rational than others because the subject can feel at home in them; the subject sees the duties and obligations of his role as properly his or her own:

> The state is the actuality of the ethical Idea – the ethical spirit as substantial will, *manifest* and clear to itself, which thinks and knows itself and implements what it knows in so far as it knows it. It has its immediate existence in *custom* and its mediate existence in the *self-consciousness* of the individual, in the individual's knowledge and activity, just as self-consciousness, by virtue of its disposition, has its *substantial freedom* in the state as its essence, its end, and the product of its activity. (§257)

Ethical life is the union of objective and subjective freedom for Hegel. It is objective because it satisfies the requirements of morality, in that it determines the duties and obligations of the subject, whereas inward individuality alone cannot. But it must also be subjective because objective freedom which is not rational and is only immediate in the reality of the subject's form of life is a blind authority which determines the subject without the moment of self-consciousness essential to full, human freedom. Such authority is external and acts as a *cause of* rather than a *reason for* action. The rationality of the state is reflected in the institutions and customs which make a critical subject possible who is able to reflect upon and recognise the rationality of the institutions. We shall return to the reflective nature of the modern subject below when we discuss antiquity contra modernity.[5]

The spheres of ethical life

So, for a state to be rational it must protect and maintain the subjective will and also allow the subject to recognise the rationality of its structures. The three spheres of ethical life – the family, civil society and the state – fulfil this dual role: one, they make it possible for the free individual subject to operate choice; and two, they allow the free individual to recognise these structures as his or her own or feel at home in them. For example, the nuclear, bourgeois family liberates the individual from dependency on the sexual drive without obstructing his personal freedom as did earlier familial structures. Similarly, civil society frees the agent from dependency on material needs.

Moreover, both institutions enforce individual rights and inform the agent of his duties in such a way that his character develops to become free and reflective: the family develops one's moral subjectivity, whereas civil society is instrumental in the formation of the agent as a discrete, particular individual with different wants from all others. Yet, civil society binds us together only through external necessity and it is the political state which imposes the demands of the good on to the egoistic individuals of the marketplace. Ethical life is immediate and natural in the family where individuals are bound by unreflective but internal ties. In civil society it is an association of individuals satisfying their needs through cooperation and we are bound to one through mutual need (the social contract version of the state, if you will). And it is made formal through the constitution of the state; or through reflective internal ties: we are bound together in a community. Taken together, they supply an identity, a sense of self in which the agent is certain of recognition by others without surrendering any of his particularity (§157).

It might be noticed that this guide is somewhat disproportionate to the series of lectures offered by Hegel himself. The majority of this book has been concerned with the theoretical underpinnings of his theory of the rational state and not the nuts and bolts of it. The third part of his lecture series, after the concept of ethical life has been developed, is concerned with the nuts and bolts: in some places a description of the actually existing Prussian state, in some places a timid prescription of how the state can be perfected. Most of these discussions the reader will be able to follow for him or herself and I shall concentrate only on what is essential or rational to the whole as such, since it is my belief that Hegel's theory is consistent with a range of states and not just the one he describes in his own series of lectures (§274R). The material in his lectures is well worth thinking about and discussing and it is perhaps more accessible to the reader who now has an idea of his language since the topics are very familiar: the structure of the family, the regulation of a capitalist market and private property, and the nature or extent of political institutions. For these reasons, what follows is nothing more than a summary.

THE FAMILY (§§158–81)

How does the structure of the family – and Hegel is explicitly concerned with the modern, bourgeois nuclear family – liberate the subject and also make possible subjective freedom? Ethical life is rational if it makes possible a space for personal freedom and can be endorsed by free subjects. The family creates interpersonality through a feeling, that is love, and love is a paradigmatic account of how I can overcome my separation and find myself *at home* in the other. The unity of love is not yet rational – as it is based on one's immediate desires – but it does supply the basis for it:

> The first moment in love is that I do not wish to be an independent person in my own right and that, if I were, I would feel deficient and incomplete. The second moment is that I find myself in another person, that I gain recognition in this person, who in turn gains recognition in me. (§158A)[6]

The use of phrase 'I find myself' coupled with the mention of recognition reveal the true relevance of the family and the bond of love for Hegel: it is an alternative to staking one's life (see Chapter 4 below). One enters into a loving marriage in order to renounce one's independence and demand recognition. The two become one, as countless love songs have wisely told us. The 'I' becomes a 'We'. And it is in the 'We' that I find myself and am certain of what I am. One can demonstrate that I would sacrifice my immediate personality and its immediate desires for someone else and thus be recognised as human through the alienable nature of my immediate, animalistic desires. It was once all the rage to go to India or to the desert to find oneself, but really when I ask myself who I truly am, all I need is the true and reliable judgement of my equal and I find an equal in someone who I love since I can trust their judgement to be for the sake of me and not disingenuous or for their own benefit (treating me as a means or an instrument of their own machinations). And my existence as a 'We' ethically frees me from egoism since self-interest is trumped by immediate altruism: my family's interests naturally come before my own and hence it is a necessary step to the purification of our immediate desires since values trump the arbitrary demands of abstract wants. My wife and children's security and future, for example, become an immediate concern to me in virtue of my natural being: 'to have self-consciousness of one's individuality *within this unity* . . . so that one is present in it not as an independent person but as a *member*' (§158). This is obvious because what 'We' want is not identical to what the two 'I's of the union want separately. (To be overly banal, I may want a sports car, my wife may want a diamond necklace, but together we may want a new conservatory – the we becomes a new particular 'I' with specific wants and interests that does not exist prior to the union of the two 'I's.)

Marriage

So, the family is a way for the ethical subject to complete him or herself and be free, and it is constituted by three elements: marriage, familial resources and children (§160). The first moment of the family is a marriage between two particular persons. In order to fully understand Hegel's picture it is worthwhile to understand what he has in his sights as a competing view, that is, any theory which professes that marriage is a contract between consenting partners whereby I agree to x (restrict my sexual partners, hold property in common, ask for consent to watch football matches, and so on) so long as you agree to reciprocal constraints (restrict your sexual partners, hold property in common, ask for consent to go shopping) (see §75R and §161A). Marriage thus conceived is a form of association for mutual benefit: in joining together the partners make compromises in order to benefit overall and if either violates the terms of the contract, all bets are off and compensation is sought. Such a view, according to Hegel is so much hogwash. For him, marriage is a legal expression of love and 'their union is a self-limitation, but since they attain their substantial self-consciousness within it, it is in fact their self-liberation' (§162). Marriage is, however, necessary, since any partnership based solely on a feeling is 'contingent' and would not supply the security necessary for complete interdependence between two persons. The problem is best illustrated by short-term cohabiting partners who, when they break up, find themselves in endless squabbles about ownership of CDs and payment of bills. Love cannot be relied upon to generate future harmony and right action. Love, then, has to be legally expressed and, as such, marriage is considered to be 'rightfully ethical love' (§161A). The recognition of this legal expression and commitment by both parties replaces the purely passion-inspired foundation of marriage and determines a new relationship of trust (§163).

Hegel outlines a little of the substantial detail of marriage. First, marriages cannot be arranged externally to the participants because not considering their views and feelings violates the right of the subjective freedom. Marriages can be arranged by parents for the endorsement by children, but there must be some inclination on the part of the individual (even if this is only to do one's familial duty and obey one's parents' wishes) so that the individual sees the action as a good for him or her (§162A). Equally, Hegel prohibits incest since it will be impossible to overcome one's immediate feeling towards the object of one's desire and hence it cannot be fully free (§168), and does allow for divorce since the basis of marriage remains passion and not pure reason (§176). However, he does introduce a rather indefensible division of sexual labour which sets man as the head of the family and woman as the hearth warmer (§§164–6); although it is hard to defend such a position it is historically understandable (even though the demand for recognition becomes asymmetrical and hence contradictory for subjective freedom).

Of greater interest is Hegel's discussion of monogamy: 'Marriage, and essentially monogamy, is one of the absolute principles on which the ethical life of a community is based' (§167R). Monogamy, one could argue, limits desire and feeling to one object and, if Hegel celebrates capitalism since it allows for the expression of subjective freedom, surely promiscuous and non-standard forms of sexuality ought also to be encouraged. Yet, for him, polygamy is an excess of love and results in obsessive destruction. Monogamy is of course more rational in terms of inheritance and property claims (an important consideration) (§178), as well as being more consistent with reciprocal equality (especially as polygamy often privileges one gender, the male), but the real reason for Hegel's defence of monogamy is that marriage is not about the arbitrary will, but the ethical will. It is the desire for recognition, to see me as I am. It might be argued that to insist this is to be carried out solely by one person seems an unnecessary limitation, for friendship may seem as likely a manifestation; but this misses the point. Marriage is the legal expression of love and love is the alternative to staking one's life. Friendship is too broad a term to describe the strength of such a relationship and has no legal form. Finally, it seems that in his insistence on heterosexual, monogamous marriage, Hegel presupposes his third respect, that of children, which we shall return to below.

The family's resources

The arbitrary acquisition of the person of abstract right is replaced, through the structure of the family, by rational acquisition for an ethical purpose (the care of what one values). The family is the first account of a rational good to be pursued by the person as opposed to the pursuit of any good (§170). Unlike abstract right whereby property is the possibility of others recognising my acts as my own, the family's resources are ethical in that they form the basis for the acquisition and care of a *community* and not just an individual.

The upbringing of children

Hegel's description of the family is fulfilled by the description of children and in the parents' role as educator and protector to children. Children are not the property of parents; they also exist for themselves. They are the objective existence of the parents' love. Property bears an external relationship to the family, whereas children are the objectification of the internal bond between parents. The parents' duty resides in the education of the children, which leads them to personhood and the dissolution of the family because in attaining personhood the child wishes to construct a new family, thus breaking his or her ties to the old (§179).

Summary of the family

The family contributes to the individual's freedom in a number of ways. First, one can overcome immediate desires through following the model of selfless unity with others; I negate my immediate desires for those of the greater good (the nobler ones). Secondly, the family promotes the greater good of lifetime commitment to one's union, thus once more supplying a model which aids one to overcome those immediate desires. Marriage liberates us from slavish attendance to the sexual drive, but it is also a commitment born from love and passion otherwise we would have no motivation (remember Hegel's comments on moral psychology here), but turns the unstable reliance on emotion into a stable form. It sets up a domestic economy of satisfaction that allows both parties to redirect sexual energy. Clearly, the structure of the family provides an immanent doctrine of duty which liberates the individual from his (or her) immediate desires and helps him to exercise his reason over the claims of the situation, his identity and his drives.

Hegel identifies three ways in which the family secures personal freedom: one, mutual recognition through love and not the struggle to death; two, through the maintenance of personhood and identity within a larger community; and, three, the overcoming of one's immediate desire in order to project a future for one's family and children. Ignoring the conservative elements of Hegel's approach to the family and also his rather romantic over-investment in love as a philosophical tool, the basic idea behind his presentation of the family is perhaps something which should not be dismissed so easily. By placing the origin of community in a *feeling* between human beings and holding that the person emerges historically posterior to this institutional structure, Hegel implicitly proposes an alternative to the more common state of nature origins of society. Instead of mutual need driving individuals together, Hegel begins from the opposite perspective: man is naturally social and only through society does he attain individuality and personhood.

Transition to civil society

Certain political writers see the family as the model for political obligation (Aristotle, 1996; Filmer, 1991). One obeys one's leader as one obeys one's father, because they know better than us and they naturally have our interests at heart. Hegel does not agree. The family differs from the state because it is not continuous, when the members leave, it dissolves. The state, on the other hand, can lose and gain members without dissolving. In his words, the members of a family are not 'accidental' to it. Moreover, the family is not self-sufficient as a household on its own could not satisfy the requirements of subjective freedom; the paths of the children and the adults would be bound to satisfying needs and not allow them that arbitrary choice necessary for full human freedom. One's future would be decided directly by one's birth and one would not be able to choose a new and different path since we are still dependent on one another.

CIVIL SOCIETY (§§182–229)

In many respects, in his description of the family Hegel is implicitly offering a pre-modern form of political union and an alternative to the dominant social contract model of the state. Instead of mutual need or necessity driving humans to cooperate, the human seeks recognition in order to be free and, hence, for the human to be fully human, he or she must be social. Civil society was often used in opposition to the state of nature, and by making it a part – and not the whole – of human relations, Hegel is acknowledging that needs and their satisfaction require cooperation whilst simultaneously denying that egoistic cooperation is the be all and end all of the state (§258R).[7] Our obligation to civil society is, indeed, motivated by egoism (to satisfy my and my family's wants), but – Hegel contends – our obligation to our state as a whole is not:

If the state is represented as a unity of different persons, as a unity which is merely a community [of interests], this applies only to the determination of civil society. Many modern exponents of constitutional law have been unable to offer any view of the state but this. In civil society, each individual is his own end, and all else means nothing to him. But he cannot accomplish the full extent of his ends without reference to others; these others are therefore means to the end of the particular [person]. But through its reference to others, the particular end takes on the form of universality, and gains satisfaction by simultaneously satisfying the welfare of others. (§182A)

Both the family and civil society foster interpersonality, but whereas the family does so from the basis of feeling, civil society relies on mutual need. The family as person is connected to other families through external and not internal bonds and this constitutes society as a cooperative response to contingency. The social will generated by the satisfaction of needs is one of cooperation with others, recognising them as persons who will consent to aid one if one is equally open to aiding them. Work and labour are the activities which produce and create the commodity as a satisfaction of a need and, hence, social labour frees us from needs.

The basic postulation of civil society can be stated thus: 'Individuals, as citizens of this state, are *private persons* who have their own interest, as their end' (§187). The mention of private persons is not a full return to abstract right and a description of rampant egoism though, for it must be remembered that these *persons* are representations of the family. Thus, the person of civil society does not pursue purely self-interested goals, but is already determined by the ethical basis of the family. A head of family takes part in civil society to further his family's interests and not solely his own. However, civil society is the objective freedom of abstract right made actual and thus the sphere in which subjective freedom has most sway and so 'where the waves of all passions surge forth' (§182A). And remember that such arbitrariness is a right of the fully free human being: civil society is the sphere of our existence in which we can best express our individuality through the selection and satisfaction of particular wants and needs. The capitalist system is, for Hegel, a necessary element of any rational state because it is the only system of needs which can allow for full and proper individual freedom.

Yet, cooperation does more. Civil society mediates between the family and the political state proper in that a commitment to cooperation will, over time, form groups and communities (the estates) which enable the subject to have an identity and to freely pursue his or her goals. The egotistical nature of the particular I is made universal through the system of needs, since cooperation generates satisfaction more so than competition and the groups that form over time to satisfy these needs make it necessary for individuals to have recourse to others, forming a way of life or community with their own needs opposed to others.

Civil society is concerned with three elements of the social system of desire-satisfaction and production: one, with the kinds of needs human beings pursue and the means by which these needs are satisfied (the system of needs); two, the protection of the individual's freedom within a the system of property and exchange (the administration of justice); and three, the regulated distribution of goods that arise through shared practices of labour so that the free market does not lead to excess or corruption (the police and corporations).

The system of needs

Hegel is, like many writers of early modernity, an apologist for the emerging capitalist economic system and the institution of private property, but his defence does not rest on more common utilitarian arguments or claims of systematic efficiency. Capitalism may well deliver what individuals want better than other systems, but – more significantly, and like Hegel's argument for private property in abstract right – it allows individuals to decide for themselves what they want. It is this implicit embodiment of freedom at the heart of capitalism that serves to justify it.[8]

One way in which human beings differ from other animals, according to Hegel, is in the relationship between the subject and his or her needs. The animal is externally determined by its needs whereas the human being is able to hold back, interrogate and dissect his desires through the use of his or her understanding. A desire may be divided into concrete parts to attain it more readily. To drink water from a murky stream, a human being need not immediately respond to the pull of his drive but can build a purifier from a tube and small stones, through which to pour the water. New desires arise in consequence: the desire to find or fashion a tube, to choose the correct stones, etc. The systematic parts of the single, immediate desire become desires in themselves. Such a banal example serves to underline the basis of the system of needs.

The fixation of needs and the means through which to attain them into a system becomes a conditioning element of civil society. For Hegel, the more needs a human has, the freer he or she is, simply because no one need can play a determinate role over him or her. Thus, the more contingent, social needs we possess, the better: 'The very multiplication of needs has a restraining influence on desire, for if people make use of many things, the pressure to obtain any one of these which they might need is less strong, and this is a sign that necessity in general is less powerful' (§190A). Thinking once more of the water purification example above, if two people were to come across the water and both desire to drink, the attainment of such a desire is most easily achieved if one collects stones whilst the other searches for or makes the tube. The co-operation displayed in civil society is based upon the desire to satisfy one's desires as quickly and effortlessly as possible, thus also serving the desires of others. It is perhaps this which best represents Hegel's appropriation of Smith's hidden hand:

In this dependence and reciprocity of work and the satisfaction of needs, *subjective selfishness* turns into a *contribution towards the satisfaction of the needs of everyone else*. By a dialectical movement, the particularity is mediated by the universal so that each individual, in earning, producing, and enjoying on his own account, thereby earns and produces for the enjoyment of others. (§199)

Commodities are increased by social production for a twofold reason: cooperation frees man from dependency on immediate necessities and also social life itself creates new needs; only in a shared community does one need a television, for example.

Cooperation in civil society leads to interpersonal existence, albeit in an external mode. Individuals must have recourse to others because they have to form a way of life or community with their own needs and modes of satisfaction in opposition to other communities as a way to increase their satisfaction. Certain groups of people with shared interests will work together recognising that they – perhaps exclusively – share a certain interest within society as a whole. Hegel identifies three main estates in modern society: one, the substantial, unreflective agriculture estate; two, the formal, individualistic estate of trade and industry; and three, the reflective, universal estate which concerns the interests of society as a whole. One could think of these as the unifying interests of farming and agriculture, business and the political, social, educational and civil workers. The members of each estate work together for their common interest in the face of the other opposing estates with differing interests (except for the last estate which consciously work for the good of all). It is a partial step towards universality since the person identifies with a greater aim than individual desire:

> The individual attains actuality entering into *existence* in general, and hence into *determinate* particularity; he must accordingly limit himself *exclusively* to one of the *particular* spheres of need. The ethical disposition within this system is therefore that of *rectitude* and the *honour of one's estate*, so that each individual, by a process of self-determination, makes himself a member of one of the moments of civil society through his activity, diligence, and skill, and supports himself in this capacity; and only through this mediation with the universal does he simultaneously provide for himself and gain *recognition* in his own eyes and in the eyes of others. (§207)

If I describe myself as a football fan, it reveals what is universal about me and may prescribe minimal formal obligations and values;

but to have 'determinate particularity', I must limit myself to a specific team: I am an Aston Villa fan. The abstract universal nature gives us formal identity, but by limiting myself exclusively to one team, I confer on myself substantial and concrete identity that is recognised simply as being 'one of them': 'When we say that a human being must be somebody, we mean that he must belong to a particular estate; for being somebody means that he has substantial being. A human being with no estate is merely a private person and does not possess actual universality' (§207A). For Hegel, the estate forms a second family and such groupings and communities will over time begin to display uniform taste, meaning and values. One will be able to recognise oneself in, say, one's taste in cinema: the descriptions of 'art house', 'mainstream', etc., are as expressive of their prospective audience as they of the film's actual content and a good sociologically based demographic would be able to predict your desires and wants on the basis of your education, job and social relations.[9]

Hegel is aware of the alienating and atomising effects of capitalism and sees the estates as a way to foster community necessary for the ordering of values and goods. More so than through the cooperative nature of civil society, it is through the estates that civil society is connected with the state as a whole. In striving for a common aim rather than a purely individual one, man allows universality into the extreme particularity of civil society. In my work I work for all *agriculturalists*, *industrialists* or *all citizens*. Again, one finds the idea of a commitment to a greater good as a liberating aspect for one's identity. The greater good of my estate confers on me the rational basis and criteria of intelligibility required for me to express my will adequately in the world:

> While the family is the primary basis of the state, the estates are the second. The latter are of special importance, because private persons, despite their selfishness, find it necessary to have recourse to others. This is accordingly the root which links selfishness with the universal, i.e. with the state, which must take care to ensure that this connection is a firm and solid one. (§201A)

The necessary division of labour in the system of needs gives rise to groups with their own lifestyles, ways and needs. And these estates have obligations to their members: to educate and develop their characters, to form the basis of rationality and allow the members to choose freely.

However, since civil society is a system of needs, production and exchange, then certain rights need to be integrated to protect freedom. Men are related as persons, thus civil society has to maintain and protect the rights of these persons. The right of subjective freedom, for example, may well be violated by the contingency of one's birth in a specific estate (I was not born into a class that considered university a viable project) and so the state must encourage the possibility of social mobility (§§206, 277). Just as abstract right required an account of wrongdoing and morality, civil society requires the administration of justice.

The administration of justice

The system of needs is the actualisation of abstract right in the sense that the right of property is both an expression of individual freedom and the worth of my life in itself; but without the means to express itself, such a right is vain and empty. The capitalist system of private property and free exchange makes possible the abstract need to possess things. Moreover, such a system needs to be policed and regulated for it – like abstract right – leads to conflict, wrongdoing and coercion. Civil society stretches beyond the limits of production and exchange: the needs of persons entail rights, thus civil society has to maintain and protect these rights for the same reason the system of abstract rights needed to be protected, viz. subjective freedom. It, therefore, requires an *administration of justice*.

And here we encounter what the title of Hegel's lecture series seems to superficially promise: a philosophy of law. Right, as I earlier stated, is a far broader term than law and covers customary behaviour, social mores and individual claims. Law, for Hegel, is the codified and solidified customs of a particular nation given existence and made actual in law:

> When what is right *in itself* is *posited* in its objective existence – i.e. determined by thought for consciousness and *known* as what is right and valid – it becomes *law*, and through this determination, right becomes *positive* right in general. (§211)

Hegel hints that very early on in a nation's history, the customs and mores of that nation will find expression as law, and it is obvious to see why. If we both claim to know what is right but the only standard of validity is in fact subjective conviction, then conflict will no doubt arise due to partiality or error. If the expectations, customs and mores of a nation are, however, written down, then recourse can be made to an official authority for judgment in the particular case. Law, to use Hegel's favourite term, is right made rational.

However, for a people to identify with the objective representation of these laws, they must be: one, clearly understood in the minds of the subjects; two, ordered and codified; and finally, open and accountable to the public domain. The first criterion reminds one of rational legitimisation found in most liberal societies, but it should not be overstated. Hegel is making the weaker claim that for a law to be valid it must be known by the subject; a woman cannot defend herself unless she knows of what she is accused and understands in what way it is a wrongdoing. The validity of the law itself, as measured by a moral conscience, is beyond the citizen's capacity since laws are merely rationalised social conventions. Hegel's view of law is a form of positivism: if the law is made by the relevant authority and it is clearly stated, then it is valid. Since such a law is transparent to consciousness and not obscure, its codification into an objective representation should pose no problem and it is for this reason Hegel requires the second criterion. It is in the third criterion that one finds the idea of a rational law:

> When right has come into existence in the form of law, it has being for-itself; as opposed to *particular volitions and opinions* with regard to itself, it is self-sufficient and has to assert itself as *universal*. This *cognition* and *actualisation* of right in the particular case, without the subjective feeling of *particular* interest, is the responsibility of a public authority, namely the *court of law*. (§219)

Law, as rational, exists for itself and can stand independently of the bodies from which it originated. Thus, for Hegel, the operations of the organs of law should be open to the public domain and accountable to the people.

Yet, there is seemingly nothing in Hegel's account that allows for protest against unjust laws. If I believe the law that prohibits smoking marijuana to be wrong, yet said law has been proposed by the proper authority and is clearly stated, then I have very little ground on which to stand. The idea of rationality for Hegel is only that a law is a proper statement of judgment and legislation, whereas customary right is not since it is susceptible to caprice and subjective partiality. Such a requirement does not rule out stupid laws (one must stand when the National Anthem plays) or immoral laws (any child born on February 29 should be sacrificed to the God of Leap Years). Hegel's response to such a claim is not yet pertinent, but he would simply state that stupid laws and 'immoral' laws would not exist since right is rational. Bad or irrational laws will not be stable, will not maintain and promote subjective freedom and so will not be the product of history. The full justification resides in his philosophy of history: laws that obstruct and violate practices of equality will eventually, given the workings of history, simply be abolished.

The Police and the Corporations

Justice exists in order that 'the livelihood and welfare of individuals should be *secured* – i.e. that *particular welfare* should be *treated as a right* and duly *actualised*' (§230). But, the administration of justice cannot exist independently of those means with which to implement it. The *police* exist as an external authority which has power over individuals' rights and can limit action in accordance with the needs of all to such an extent that it may, in grave circumstances, stand in for and take over from the family (§239). As such, the word 'police' is best thought of in its present participle form as in the phrase 'policing the state', and would be best understood as an umbrella term for the police proper, social services, watchdogs, commissions, public standards bodies, local councils, etc. (§236A).

If the three estates were the general delineation of a modern society, the corporations exist to represent the interests of more specific groups within such a divisional structure concerned with the trade and industry estate since these individuals are most likely to pursue their interests in a dangerously self-centred way: the miners, the stock brokers, etc. The *corporations* determine that the ethical remains a priority in civil society as an immanent principle and are peculiar to the second estate alone since '. . . it has the right to assume the role of a second family for its members, a role which must remain more indeterminate in the case of civil society in general, which is more remote from individuals and their particular requirements' (§252). As such, the corporations give support to their members through looking after their interests, recruiting new members, protecting members against contingency (famine, injury, etc.) and providing training and education. Corporations are a naive mix of business lobbyists, guilds and unions, where Hegel rather optimistically believes all will share the same interest: the idea being that happy workers are good workers, and productive workers generate good returns and are rewarded deservedly. Hegel is perhaps too optimistic in buying into this aspect of capitalist justification: managers and workers will often be alienated from one another, rather than – perhaps the Japanese model – seeing some greater good in their service to the company or vocation. Together the police and corporations consist of all those agencies needed if subjects are to attain that which they want from the state by ensuring contracts are kept, educating their members and through the control of poverty. The police also supply an infrastructure which meets the basic needs of people so that poverty can be remedied as far as possible, through education, health services, financial support and the reinforcing of a man's duty to his family, not unlike a modern welfare state (§§239–240).

Hegel demonstrates an astute and unexpected sensitivity for the contingent evils of capitalism: poverty and the atomism of civil society. Capitalism ensures recognition as a free particular individual, but it needs to be regulated otherwise it undermines the 'homeliness' of the state and leads to social atomism. He is well aware that external factors well outside of the sphere of control of an individual can take away his or her livelihood: say the discovery of a new fuel technology that replaces the burning of coal hitting the livelihood of miners, or the importing of cars from cheaper and more efficient labourers abroad undermining home production. The administration of justice is enforced through a policing of the state by a public authority which controls the worst excesses of civil society, and the corporations which inject an ethical element into the members' lives of the estate of trade and industry. Such a policing ensures that extravagance, excess and poverty are avoided even though they appear inherently connected to civil society under capitalism. Hegel is right to resist these vices, simply because they lead to the dissolution of community and the violation of subjective freedom.

First, poverty dehumanises man. It opens him up to the will of others as their 'means merely', he becomes the vehicle of an alien will so that he may survive and is reduced to a status no better than the slaves. Yet, whatever the moral ills of poverty, Hegel is equally concerned with the real political problem of the dehumanised men forming a mass which may threaten the stability of the state:

When a large mass of people sinks below the level of a certain standard of living . . . that feeling of right, integrity, and honour which comes from supporting oneself by one's own activity and work is lost. This leads to the creation of a *rabble*, which in turn makes it much easier for disproportionate wealth to be concentrated in a few hands. (§244)

The consequence of massive inequality leads to the danger of revolution and Hegel is well aware that when a workforce is no longer engaged in labour then it presents a problem to the state for whereas a man cannot truly seek recompense against a volcano eruption, he does see his fellow countrymen as owing him something and begins to resent those who still have wealth when his or hers has been lost. The impoverishment of the proletariat turns them into a rabble, depriving them of culture and turning them against society as a whole. Hegel's solution is first a recourse to the security of estates and corporations who look after their members and then, failing this, colonisation in order to displace the rabble.

Second, for all civil society's aspirations to universality, it is based on the energetic motivation of self-interest. Such self-interest should be curbed because man can so easily blind himself to the claims of unity and universality, thus dissolving the true aim of the state. Atomism – or the alienation of human being from human being – is an evil since, if civil society becomes too powerful, it will swallow the ethical sphere completely and lead to the dissolution of the state (§236R). No one will care about the universal community, only one's personal interests which will lead to chaos and poverty. As such, Hegel proposes an infrastructure that is aimed at securing the freedom of the rational will through the sustenance of a system which protects those contingent, yet actual, states of affairs which compromise it. Capitalism is the most rational way for the subjective will to express its particularity, yet it is also an ever-present danger to its existence.

Summary of civil society

The family fostered interpersonality immediately through unreflective feeling. Civil society fosters interpersonality based on external bonds between persons. It does so through a system of needs which divides labour and leads to community through the cooperation of specialist workers who indirectly work for the good of society as a whole. More significantly, the division of labour creates 'estates' whereby persons adhere to a whole of which they are but a member and this is the ethical element of universality present in the system of needs since, as with the family, it proposes a commitment through which persons can overcome the claims of the immediate situation. Therefore, civil society has to make provision for the correct and rational running of the system of needs. This is achieved through an administration of justice in which each person can appeal to his rights as a bearer of rational will. The rights of the system of needs become positive law and in positive law the equality and common aim of all men is secured.

Civil society makes desire itself the determining factor of humanity, thus it supplements the universality of family life with the particularity of the claims of needs. Since it is built on the satisfaction of needs, both necessary and contingent desires become determined by their possible satisfaction. Civil society creates external recognition: I recognise you as other pursuing your ends which may or may not coincide with my own. Civil society is the state of necessity and, since it is built on the satisfaction of needs, it is desire itself rather than the content of these desires which determines the system. Such a mentality must be controlled otherwise it will lead to extravagance, excess and poverty; those things which remove humanity from the human through the re-creation of the master in extravagance who can no longer recognise *his* will in the world, instead relying on the excess of the arbitrary will, and the re-creation of the *slave* in poverty who becomes the vehicle of an alien will just to survive (§185).

Having described the structure of Hegel's civil society and in what ways it secures personal freedom, I shall add only a single critical point (but there are others) on whether his description is as rational as he assumes. I shall not stress the peculiar nature of his account nor its conservatism; rather, one thing concerns me: the role of the 'estates'. Hegel stresses that there is to be mobility through the 'estates' and it is obvious that this is required for personal freedom. Yet it is not clear how this is possible. One is born a land worker or an industrial worker. One is educated and cared for by one's estate. It seems that the rigid estate system Hegel puts in place privileges the rational, objective nature of the state over the personal freedom of the individual. It seems that the demand for subjective freedom is lost in the actual machinations of civil society. I leave the reader to think this comment through.

'THE POLITICAL STATE PROPER AND ITS CONSTITUTION' (§§272–340)[10]

Before discussing the theoretical underpinnings of the rational state as a whole, it is worthwhile first to proceed to the structure and institutions of the political state proper and its 'internal constitution', or what we might commonly call the government and its organs. Much of what Hegel discusses is interesting and very relevant to political science, but it is too vast to adequately discuss here. There is also the question of relevance. He is describing a particular constitution of a particular nation and admits others may be different for contingent reasons as long as the foundations of the constitution are rational (§274R). This is a further reason I feel confident to look mainly at the foundations and not the details; I shall only concentrate on the state as a form of objective freedom that maintains and promotes recognition and personal freedom. What follows is the barest of sketches since the reader will be able to understand most of Hegel's own discussions for him or herself.

The power of the sovereign

The objective existence of the state has three elements; one, the legislative power; two, the executive power; and three, the power of the sovereign (§273). Hegel begins with the third determination of the political state and it is convenient to follow his lead simply because it allows us to grasp in its entirety the structure of the state. He envisages it as a constitutional monarchy and when he talks of the sovereign he has in mind a hereditary monarch. The role of the sovereign is to conclude the deliberation of the other powers and their constituent parts by giving the ultimate and final decision on political discussion, thus being the ultimate court of appeal (§§279, 284). Basically, as Hegel himself notes, the role of the sovereign in a rational and strong constitution will be to cross the t's and dot the i's (§§279A, 280A). However, over and above this, Hegel identifies particular offices such as the appointment of higher civil servants (§§283, 292) and the right to pardon (§282).

Why, though, should the sovereign be a monarch rather than a body of people or, in fact, all the people? Hegel's answer is that a state run by institutions, conglomerates or companies is anonymous and alien to its subjects and is able to deflect criticism on to whomever of the company fitted the bill. A minion would often be scapegoated, whereas with a personal sovereign, the buck must stop with him as person (§284). Hegel does not make the monarch accountable, however. It is not the case that the sovereign can be dismissed if things do not go well. Rather, the monarch reflects the personhood of the people as a whole: if things are bad, who should we blame? The answer would seem to be ourselves, the people, for decision and deliberation has to do with the estates and corporations who form the laws and constitution. These, in turn, reflect the will of their members and the sovereign's role is to ratify these decisions.

Hegel argues that such a sovereign must be a hereditary monarch. He is against republicanism for good reasons: one, a president elected either by the people or the representatives of the people will be bound to the legislative powers and not above them and, hence, any decision taken by this person would never be truly final; it can be overthrown whenever he is replaced. And two, the elected sovereign would be incapable of unifying all the members of the state since he or she will probably reflect the interests of a faction. A monarch is advantageous because he or she remains independent of the organs of the state: '. . . ultimate self-determination can fall within the sphere of human freedom only in so far as it occupies this supreme position, *isolated for itself* and exalted *above everything particular* and *conditional*; for only thus does its actuality accord with its concept' (§279R).

Hegel offers a reasonable enough argument for the independence of the sovereign but fails to justify the hereditary principle. He tries to appeal to 'naturalness': although, originally, an arbitrary accident of birth or political upheaval, the monarch can now be justified simply by tradition (§280). More importantly than the absence of a real argument for the hereditary principle (other than it is the best of bad alternatives), there seemingly exists an immanent problem with the idea concerning the subjective freedom of the poor soul destined to be monarch. His or her career is not open to talents, neither has he the right to exercise his arbitrary will (although the second in line historically makes up for this lack) and, it seems, at least one member of the rational state is not fully free.

The executive power

The executive power consists of civil servants who restrict the power of civil society by bringing particular interests into line with the universal good by the execution of legislature. These civil servants are free from immediate necessity so that they can find their satisfaction in the performance of their duties: 'The civil servant is not employed, like an agent, to perform a single contingent task, but makes this relationship [to his work] the main interest of his spiritual and particular existence' (§294R). Every citizen has the right to become a civil servant and Hegel keeps the career open to talents and does so wisely so that the universal class will not be populated by one interest group (§277, although contrast with §§283 and 292).

The legislative power

The legislative power is concerned with the formation and determination of the laws of the state that are ratified by the sovereign and implemented by the executive (§300). The executive plays an advisory role on the concrete consequences of a specific law, explaining how the law may affect the day-to-day running of, say, the social services, but the deliberations must be carried out by the legislature. And since laws must represent the interests of citizens and also enforce the rationality of the state itself, Hegel proposes the estates as the perfect organ for the legislature:

> Viewed as a *mediating* organ, the Estates stand between the government at large on the one hand and the people in their division into particular spheres and individuals on the other. Their determination requires that they should embody in equal measure both the *sense* and *disposition* of the *state* and *government* and the *interests of particular* circles and *individuals*. (§302)

It is through the estates that the interests of individuals have an effect on the legislative process. The individual voice is kept out of the political process since, according to Hegel, it is the interest or estate which is relevant to political decision: an individual as a private person has no concrete interests (the private person is characterised as 'wanting' not 'wanting that'), but as a member of an estate an individual has substantial identity and concrete interests that can be promoted or obstructed by law (§308R). And since these interests will be shared by all members of the estate, they can be represented by the estate (§311R). So, rather than propose democratic participation in government, the relationship between individuals and the state is mediated by the estates. The estates as a new super-person protect their members through playing a role in the formation of those external laws which are determinate on individuals and they also communicate both the interests of their members to the government and, reciprocally, the reasoning of the government to its members so that families and individuals can see why they ought to act according to the dictates of the state when they may come into conflict with self-interest.

The assembly of the legislature is divided into two houses: the first represents the estate of natural ethical life, landed property and family life so the interests of the family will be reflected. (The universal estate is represented in the executive.) This first house will be populated by those members who hold property rights or titles and does not differ substantially from the pre-reformed House of Lords. The second represents civil society and will be constituted by deputies who represent specific corporations and their interests. The two houses will be public to raise awareness of universal interests and also to control the power of the sovereign so that he is not alienated from his people; to control interests of communities, corporations and individuals; and to ensure that individuals do not become a mass power in opposition to the state.

Summary of the political state proper

Interpersonality is guaranteed on three levels: one, the family, through unreflective, internal bonds of feeling; two, civil society, through external bonds of co-operation and identity in membership of an estate; and three, the state itself, through internal, reflective bonds which allow the person to recognise the family and the estate bound in one concrete identity which is the rational life. Hegel sketches the organisation of a state which has the aim of unifying the people into one identity. The political state proper limits the excesses of civil society which threaten to alienate people from one another and it also mediates between the interests of an estate and the unity of the state. Such a brief description of the central elements of Hegel's account of the state does not do justice to the intricacy or subtleties of his extensive discussions, nor does it really pose the question of how far he is merely proposing a conservative agenda. Even if such a description would become necessarily controversial, I would say that the account of the state is ultimately disappointing: we find that the estates override individual concerns and that that the principle of hereditary monarchy is counter to subjective freedom. Furthermore, the lack of any real democratic accountability or participation is also counter to subjective freedom. Surely, like capitalism, democracy is a necessary evil for the expression of the subjective will.

THE HISTORICAL JUSTIFICATION OF THE STATE

Two ideal worlds (§§341–60)

Hegel holds that the writings of thinkers who belong to the social contract tradition reflects something peculiarly distinctive about modern society brought about by the Reformation in Europe. The emergence of the particular 'I' is no longer a theoretical element of the rational state but an historical event: subjective freedom, liberated from blind obedience to authority, demands that the state be justified in a way that is transparent. Prior to the Reformation, the priests could command the people with a simple shrug of the shoulders and a 'who can understand God's ways, even if I am better placed than you?', and leaders could be sure in their authority due to the common assumption of a natural qualitative chain of being amongst men. However, post-Reformation Europe demanded that all men were equal under God and the world began to enter the age of reason. We have continually wondered in this book how Hegel can, on the one hand, celebrate the necessary element of the subjective will in the modern state, and yet, on the other hand, seemingly propose that the standards of objectivity of right are to be derived from the existing state (§261A). The fragile balance between subjective and objective freedom rests at the heart of his enterprise. Rather than diligently examine the details of his account of the state to show how subjective freedom is either promoted or inhibited, it is more pertinent to conclude with a discussion of how he systematically believes that the 'hard struggle between these two realms' can be reconciled (§360). The answer is, as has often been hinted, through history.

For Hegel, the destiny of freedom is more or less the passage from one almost rational world to the rational world; or from Ancient Greece to modern society. Greek and modern society, according to Hegel, share an important structural arrangement in that human desires accord with human nature: the structures of the family, the economy and the political state lead to the purification of the subject's natural drives along rational lines. Yet, Greece was only *almost* perfect since its inhabitants lacked self-consciousness, they acted before an objective rule of heaven and not from natures recognised as their own: 'the ultimate decision of the will is not yet assigned to the subjectivity of self-consciousness which has being for itself, but to a power which stands above and outside it . . .' (§356). Subjective freedom was not recognised: the Greeks accepted the truth of the community's values and did not question their validity.

The ideal society is one in which the form of life is not only noncorruptive but is also appropriated as *mine*. It is freely and rationally legitimised; it becomes rational not only *in itself* but also *for itself*. This is the end of history in which once again man's needs, although diversified and strengthened through self-consciousness, accord with the community's values through the organisation man is able to give himself through self-determination within the questioned limits of the values of a form of life. In both Greece and the modern world, human values and desires originate in the state and find their justification in the state. Yet, in the Greek world, man expressed his nature unknowingly: his actions were the expression of the good and the true, but were not essentially his: 'The individual will of the Subject adopts unreflectively the conduct and habit prescribed by Justice and the Laws. The individual is therefore in unconscious unity with the Idea – the social weal' (VPG, 106–7). He adds in the same text that, for the Greeks:

> The substance [the Principle] of Justice, the common weal, the general interest, is the main consideration; but it is so only as

Custom, in the form of Objective Will, so that morality properly
so called – subjective conviction and intention – has not yet man-
ifested itself. Law exists, and is in point of substance, the Law of
Freedom – rational [in its form and purport] and valid *because it
is Law*, i.e. without ulterior sanction. As in Beauty the Natural
element – its sensuous coefficient – remains, so also in this customary morality, laws assume the form of a necessity of Nature.
(VPG, 251–2)

In contrast, in modern society, reason expresses the essential nature
of man as freedom in unifying the self and the world through action
which man *recognises* as his because he expresses his subjective will
as an element independent of the dictates of the state.

However, here arises the problem. The modern subject differs
from the Greek subject in that he wants his end for himself as well
as it being a duty or dictate of his ethical life. So, he might say: 'I
want to be compassionate if I am to be a good father and it is merely
a coincidence that, in my society, the objective determinations of the
family and its values makes such comportment possible. Therefore,
I happily feel at home in such structures.' But, of course, given that
Hegel is promoting an immanent rather than a radical critique of
social structures, and believes the latter to be impossible, such a subjective conscience arises from the customs and habits of the state.
Surely every individual in history would have made the same judgement concerning the immediate and mediate dictates of his or her
own specific society. Once more, relativism raises its head.

The life of the state (§§257–71)

Hegel does not swim against the main tide of Enlightenment thought
simply to play the conservative or to ingratiate himself to his political masters. His position is far more subtle. Hegel recognises that the
subject requires the harmony of the ancient world because the particular will of the individual cannot be the standard of legitimacy:
'The determinations of the will of the individual acquire an objective
existence through the state, and it is only through the state that they
attain their truth' (§261A). Values, duties and rational institutions
cannot be derived *a priori* from individual reason since the arbitrariness of the subjective will leads to the Terror of revolutions and the
excesses of civil society. He sees this as the consequence of socially

atomistic thinking and he recognises that the individual requires a network of meanings, values and reasons to be fully rational. Yet, this network cannot determine the will just due to its existence, as it did in the Greek world where it was seen as divine, because the subjective will demands it finds its satisfaction in the action:

> The principle of modern states has enormous strength and depth because it allows the principle of subjectivity to attain fulfilment in the *self-sufficient extreme* of personal particularity, while at the same time *bringing it back to substantial unity* and so preserving this unity in the principle of subjectivity itself. (§260)

We here find a repetition of the concerns of metaphysical freedom at the political level. (See Chapter 4 above.) Full human freedom has to meet two constraints: the subjective and the objective. In modern society, as in the Greek world, the agent's subjective wants coincide with and accord with his form of life's value. However, more than this, the agent must be aware of his (or her) wants as *his* and not just a determination of the will supplied by his community. The question remains as to how successful Hegel is at meeting his own dual-faceted demand.

The demand is supposedly met through the modern, nuclear family, through a capitalist system of distribution and the institution of private property, and through the political state proper. All three spheres together form the rationality of the state as a whole. It is in the rational state as a whole that the human gains full recognition and meaning since, through it, he (or she) can satisfy the subjective criterion of freedom because he recognises the laws as rationally – internally – binding on his will: 'The state in and for itself is the ethical whole, the actualisation of freedom, and it is the absolute end of reason that freedom should be actual' (§258A). The political state proper is, then, that which makes transparent the universal element of private persons in their activity which is directed towards a common and not just self-interested end. It is in the state that the people recognise the police and corporations as their own through political affiliation and connection. As Hegel puts it:

> Individuals as a mass are themselves spiritual natures, and they therefore embody a dual moment, namely the extreme of *individuality* which knows and wills *for itself*, and the extreme of

universality which knows and wills the substantial. They can therefore attain their right in both of these respects only in so far as they have actuality both as private and as substantial persons. In the spheres in question [i.e. family and civil society], they attain their right in the first respect directly; and in the second respect, they attain it by discovering their essential self-consciousness in [social] institutions as that *universal* aspect of their particular interests which has being in itself, and by obtaining through these institutions an occupation and activity directed towards a universal end within a corporation. (§264)

A person is both individual, as the rational will for itself, and universal, as the substantial, rational element reflected in his or her history, culture and social institutions. Reason and freedom are not actualised in the pursuit of individual desires, since this is just the element of absolute freedom and terror; the extreme of individuality. Freedom and reason are actualised in the pursuit of common goals in which individuals find themselves recognised by others and recognise their identity in the common identity (be it the estate, corporation, family or, as is most common, a mixture of these).

The subjective existence of the state lies in the recognition of one's identity as properly one's own and a feeling of homeliness in the state. Such recognition is exhibited as 'in general is one of *trust* (which may pass over into more or less educated insight)' which, politically, exhibits itself as patriotism:

> The political *disposition*, i.e. *patriotism* in general, is certainly based on *truth* . . . and a volition which has become *habitual*. As such, it is merely a consequence of the institutions within the state, a consequence in which rationality is *actually* present, just as rationality receives its practical application through action in conformity with the state's institutions. (§268)

In his remark, Hegel is at pains to distance patriotism from any flag-waving barbarism, but identify it as a mere confidence that the leaders and executors of one's community embody the will of oneself.[11] Once more the individual is liberated from having to generate *ex nihilo* the idea of what to do, or having to rationally justify each dictate of right. (Should I drive on the left today? Should I thank the person for holding the door open? And so on.) One cannot be sure that a particular law is necessary for personal freedom, yet one can be sure if it is the product of the development of the free and rational state, then it more than likely is. Reflective trust forms the disposition necessary for social harmony and, perhaps rightly, only certain states will be able to rely on the trust of their citizens rather than on more repressive instruments of compliance. Harmony is ensured by the coincidence of the subjective will and the objective determinations that make such a will possible:

> What matters most is that the law of reason should merge with the law of particular freedom, and that my particular end should become identical with the universal; otherwise, the state must hang in the air. It is the self-awareness of individuals which constitutes the actuality of the state, and its stability consists in the identity of the two aspects in question. (§265A)

In other words, only through surpassing my particular interests and desires, and investing my self in a common identity which grants me recognition in the face of others who know and validate my actions, can I truly be both formally and substantially free. Only if the state is 'lived' does it have authority over a people, that is, only if they can recognise the validity of its claims on them do people respect the authority of the state.

And this life of the state, for Hegel, entails that it exists over and above its parts or the individuals that constitute it. Just as the association of Aston Villa supporters continues to exist even if its members change, but cannot exist without any members at all, so too does the state have a life. Hegel is once more placing himself against the predominant timbre of his time. The social contract tradition implicitly incorporates the scientific spirit of the Enlightenment in its attempt to reduce the state to its constituent parts (individuals) and describe the laws that govern these parts. The state is, for Hegel, more akin to a large organism: it grows, it develops and it changes. Above all, it has an aim: freedom. And since it has a purpose, we can describe one state as better than another or one institution as more rational than another if it makes the attainment of this aim more possible. Hence, Hegel's critique of the state will be immanent and not radical; he will not measure it against given goods such as liberty or equality, but ask whether the state makes full human freedom possible understood as harmony and homeliness.

History and what is

The worry remains that Hegel is guilty of describing only what happens to be the case in the Prussian state and not living up to his own standard of immanent critique. Such a judgement would only be partially true, though. Why is it that Hegel is ruled so strongly by 'what is'? Why is the denouement of the *Philosophy of Right* ultimately a conservative account of the state? A clue can be found by returning to the Preface (Hegel told us that 'philosophy forms a circle' (§2A)): even philosophers cannot transcend their time and one's thinking is necessarily bound to that tradition to which one is accountable. Hegel's description of 'what is' may simply be the implicit acceptance of this fact.

It does not, however, consign the thinker to a passive role. The laws of the state and the mores of one's tradition are rational, but only proximately so. The thinking mind must make them actually rational as their rationality is hidden and obscured by the method of their presentation. When the mother tells her son: 'Don't pull faces because if the wind changes you will stay like that', the rationality of the command is implicit. One could say that it is rational in itself. The thinking mind takes the command and attempts to strip away the presentation to reveal its truth: that the child needs to learn the appropriate behaviour for specific situations. The customary manner in which the prescription is given and the superstition in which it is incorporated only motivate because the child has a trust in his or her mother, but the rationality is for itself, it can stand free of its presentation or its givenness and when the child recognises the 'why' of his mother's words rather than just their imperative nature, the command is in and for itself rational. Reason actualises itself through the proximate given values and meanings of society becoming apparent, transparent and rational, and when this happens the subject *comprehends*. In modern society, there exists the possibility for the subject to comprehend which was not present in Greek society.

Hegel offers a critical rather than a revolutionary Enlightenment stand. The 'given' is to be rationalised not overthrown, authority is to be questioned rather than rejected. In stressing the comprehension of the given, Hegel is recognising the need for citizens to be reason-able to their tradition even though they are engaged in the project of making the truth rational. The accusation remains that Hegel's sub-stantial account of the state is too conservative and, although this in itself is not a crime, his conservatism violates his own formal require-ments as laid out in the first half of the *Philosophy of Right*. Given Hegel's belief that 'what is' is rational, he himself would have no problem with such an accusation. However, the actual state exists above the real state: actuality is not reality. Neither is it the dreams of utopians or idealists. Actuality refers to the modification of the real to make it rational: 'Rational, practical people do not let them-selves be impressed by what is possible, precisely because it is only possible; instead they hold onto what is actual – and, of course, it is not just what is immediately there that should be understood as actual' (EL, §143A). Actuality is the possibility of the maximum rationalisation of that which historically exists. Thus, the mother's command is actually true in that it appeals to another truth rather than the metamorphic power of a wind-bitten face; it appeals to the need to show respect to others and behave in ways that cannot be mis-interpreted. Its actuality resides in the being made apparent of its true, hidden rationality. Thus, actuality is both reasonableness to one's historical tradition and a simultaneous making apparent the rational nature of that which historically exists. Actuality is the best approximation to truth and rationality given the constraints of one's present, historical condition.

Is the accusation that Hegel is too influenced by historical con-tingency valid given what has just been said concerning actuality? I think the answer to this remains yes. Although one cannot magic rational kingdoms out of the air with a simple incantation of 'it ought to be thus', Hegel describes what is in reality rather than in actuality. Abstract right as the metaphysical basis of the state is too thin a concept to create laws. Hegel charts the failures of strategies which have attempted to devise and create laws on the basis of moral freedom, subjectivism, etc. (§141). Ethical life, for him, is the sub-stantial element of any moral norms or state laws and philosophy seeks to make actual the rationality implicit in the structures and practices of these institutions. The concepts which fall out of abstract right can only be applied to that which they encounter in reality. One cannot use them as a blueprint with which to build a state from the top down. One must ask in what way is the actuality of the state to be made apparent; personal freedom can only over-come a system and not create one from scratch.[12] However, this does not mean one is bound to one's time, actualisation is the overcoming of that which is not rational in reality: '. . . a contingent existence does not deserve to be called something-actual in the emphatic sense of the word; what contingently exists has no greater value than that which something-possible has; it is existence which (although it is) can just as well not be' (EL, §6R). Reason made actual overcomes the contingency in one's *Sittlichkeit*.

Hegel's confidence rests on an assumption: that what exists is inherently rational. In the past, societies have institutionalised slavery and practised human sacrifice. Why is it that the modern subject can exhibit such trust in the structures and institutions of society that he need not demand radical change only modification to contingent factors arising over time? The answer to that lies in the ultimate justification of the modern state: history or, as Hegel characterises it borrowing from Schiller, 'the world's court of judgement' (§340). The destiny of the state is human freedom and any institution or practice which is inimical to human freedom will, through the grinding mill of history, be worn away. Slavery cannot survive because the freedom of the slaves is required as much by the masters as it is by the slaves. Practices that violate the abstract rights of property and physical integrity will not be permitted post-Reformation. In a very Protestant vein, history makes a heaven on Earth through the reconciliation of the subjective and objective aspects of the will in a rational state (§360). Hegel's story of progress is only briefly outlined in the last few paragraphs of the *Philosophy of Right* but it is by its plausibility that the validity of his conservatism either stands or falls. Unfortunately, that is another book.[13]

Study Questions

1. Is it possible for the subject to appraise and judge his or her obligations, social roles and the values of his or her ethical life?
2. Why is the notion of progress so fundamental to Hegel's political philosophy? Can Hegel prove that social and political institutions are progressing?

CHAPTER 8

RECEPTION AND INFLUENCE

THE LONELINESS OF THE LONG-DISTANCE HEGEL READER

There was a time, no so long ago, when one tended to shuffle around philosophy departments in the UK like Peter hoping no one would pin you down with the words: 'You. You're one of them, I saw you with them. You're a Hegelian, aren't you?' Such an atmosphere has changed a little as Hegel has had some of the respect he rightfully deserves restored to him, but he is a figure that manages to produce a reaction even if one is unaware of what he actually wrote (and this is true even of professional philosophers who are usually more cautious). Those who haven't read him (and have no intention of doing so) generally hold his thought to be not much better than that of a mystical charlatan and his work a collection of invented neologisms and opaque prose. And those who read him religiously tell us that if we do not invest the time required to understand him, then all the worse for us. The truth, as always, lies somewhere in between. What is interesting is that Hegel has always divided opinion in this manner, from the first accusations of Schopenhauer, through to the ringing, yet so badly corrupted, endorsement of Giovanni Gentile. It is true that the obscure style of expression and the personalised vocabulary allow interpreters to commit the equivalent of philosophical murder with the ever-present alibi of the claim that true understanding can only be gained by comprehending his metaphysical system as a whole. And it is equally true that Hegel is often guilty of obfuscating difficult arguments with jargon when the going gets tough. What cannot be denied is that the history of philosophy would not have been the same without him.

IMMEDIATE INFLUENCE

The immediate reception of Hegel's *Philosophy of Right* was far from favourable due in no small part to his flagrant and intemperate criticism of Fries which was perceived to be an endorsement of the state's repressive educational policy, yet was more than probably personal spite. Such a reactionary reading of Hegel gave rise to many right-wing supporters who saw his philosophy, and the political element especially, as the grounds for halting reform and returning to reactionary policies. Tellingly, his own students – Eduard Gans among them – adopted more of a centrist reading, advocating a form of critical conservatism and reformism: it is best to stick with what we have and reform it slowly from within.

More famously, though, were the next generation of students, the so-called Young Hegelians – Feuerbach (1804–72), Marx (1818–83) and Engels (1820–95), the most famous amongst them – who attempted to develop Hegelian themes into a radical critique of society, most famously expressed in Marx's claim to have turned Hegel on his head:

> Morality, religion, metaphysics, all the rest of ideology, and their corresponding forms of consciousness, thus no longer retain the semblance of independence. They have no history, no development; but men, developing their material production and their material intercourse, alter, along with this their real existence, their thinking and the products of their thinking. Life is not determined by consciousness, but consciousness by life. (Marx, 1977c, 164)

This quotation, in many ways, captures the significance of Marx's attack on idealism and its relationship to value. All non-scientific discourse – and we should be careful to note that scientific for Marx means articulated in the language of historical materialism – is merely a symptom, an effect or a production of deeper material relations between classes defined in economic terms. In the last sentence, we are given a version of the phrase: 'The mode of production of material life conditions the general process of social, political and intellectual life. It is not the consciousness of men that determines their existence, but their social existence that determines their consciousness' (Marx, 1977d, 389). This statement expresses the foundation of

Marx's anti-Hegelian stance: for he, perhaps unfairly, read Hegel as believing the motor of history was the ideas of men, that the ideas of men changed social and political systems, whereas for Marx it is vice versa: the economic system, the material relations between men, determines our ideas, our beliefs and produces our ideology.

However, it is interesting to note that Hegel is somewhat more encompassing than Marx. For Marx no doubt had a better understanding of the impact industrialisation had on the lives of individuals, whereas Hegel initially, in the *Phenomenology of Spirit*, saw the ideas of the Reformation and the French Revolution (expressions of *Geist*) as the motor of change. However, by the time of his Berlin lectures on right and political philosophy, Hegel's picture was far more complex. The social world as a whole, which includes its economic relations, structural arrangements, historical formation, its religious and moral traditions, and geographical identity, determines the beliefs and concepts of human beings. All these elements form a web that constitutes a person's and a society's self-understanding. Marx presents a more vertical hierarchy: the ground of all change and social phenomena is and remains the economic structure of a community and though (as strange as the next phrase will sound) his vision is perhaps simpler, the Hegelian conception is more plausible. Just as with the debate between Kant and Hegel, it is not so much Hegel *or* Marx, but perhaps Hegel *and* Marx.

The brunt of the debate between Marx and Hegel does not lie in the choice between dialectics and historical materialism, but rather in a shared aspiration: the reconciliation of the human being with itself. For Hegel, modern society with its institutions of the bourgeois family, private property and capitalism, and a constitutional state would bring about this reconciliation. For Marx, capitalism and private property alienate man and inhibit reconciliation (and his critique of Hegel is at its most telling when he deals with empirical rather than metaphysical concerns). Marx is as concerned with self-determination as Hegel: for an action to be the expression of human freedom as opposed to animalistic instinct (being bound to one's immediate desires) or the unfree determination of a social system (working in a factory), the agent who creates must, first, view what he produces as worthwhile and valuable to him and others; and, second, know that it is his free choice to produce it. These are the subjective conditions labour must meet in order to be free. The objective conditions are those of the system of material labour which would make such freedom possible: the labourer must subjectively endorse the system of values that his society promotes and also participate in the decision-making processes which determine which goods are to be produced. Marx's concern, contra Hegel, is that capitalism and private property obstruct human freedom and alienate human beings.

HISTORICAL IMPACT ON THE PHILOSOPHICAL TRADITION

After Hegel's influence declined in Germany, it began to take root in other European countries. It would be no exaggeration to state that every European country had its moment of Hegelian idealism and the inevitable counter-movement. In Britain, Hegel's influence was instrumental in the practical and social philosophy of, most prominently, T. H. Green (1836–82), F. H. Bradley (1846–24) and Bernard Bosanquet (1848–1923). In Italy, Hegelian idealism inspired the aesthetics and historicism of Benedetto Croce (1866–1952) and, more notoriously, the enthusiastic Giovanni Gentile's (1875–1944) theoretical justifications of Mussolini's fascism.

It was perhaps in France that the revival of Hegel's philosophical system made most impact. The lectures of both Aleksandr Kojève (1902–68) and Jean Hyppolite (1907–69) inspired the first generation of major twentieth-century French thinkers. Just as Søren Kierkegaard (1813–55) had in his isolation sought to resist the dominant 'Hegelian' system with an avowal of the authenticity of individual experience, so, too, did the French reintroduction of Hegelian doctrines lead to an emergence of an anti-rationalist existentialism, perhaps most famously expressed in the works of Georges Bataille (1897–1962) and Jean-Paul Sartre (1905–80). The latter's thought, indeed, owed a great debt to Hegel, and Sartre's claim in his later life that Marxism is the only philosophy of our time is both disingenuous and the fruit of a long (and vain) attempt to articulate an ethics of authenticity grounded in the Hegelian concept of recognition (Sartre, 1991). One need only skim through his *Notebooks for an Ethics* to understand the urgency that Sartre exhibits in his desire to conceptualise an interpersonal relationship between human beings based on Hegelian recognition in order to replace the earlier Hobbesian political vision of *Being and Nothingness.*.

Hegelian social philosophy once more came to the forefront of German thought with the members of the Frankfurt School of

Critical Theory – Max Horkheimer (1895–1973), Theodor Adorno (1903–69) and Herbert Marcuse (1898–1979) – where the theme of immanent rationality was fused with Marx's materialism in order to produce a critique of society. Much of our contemporary Jürgen Habermas's (1929–) revival of social normativity through communicative ethics can be understood as a non-idealist Kantian response to the Hegelian critiques of transcendental moralities.

CONTEMPORARY RELEVANCE

Recently, Hegel's social philosophy has undergone a further revival in the UK and North America. Not only is there interest in what the *Philosophy of Right* can bring to the debating table on the problems of contemporary political philosophy, but it also offers us an account of political justification that is, on the surface, compatible with liberalism, but relies on a justificatory framework to which many liberals would be hostile. Hegel's description of the state may well be too reactionary for some, but there is little doubt that, in the pages of the *Philosophy of Right*, the rational state will have to embody the central values of liberty, equality and individual welfare; the very values of modern liberalism. However, Hegel's philosophy is not a simple realist avowal of these values, but a demonstration of why they are, in fact, of value at all. He outlines a justification of the bourgeois liberal state which avoids the irrationality and preference-satisfaction reliance of many liberal theories which seem to exacerbate the very real problems of social atomism and alienation. Hegel does not take rights or the value of the individual as his starting point, but instead justifies them as necessary elements of a rational state if the subject is to feel 'at home' in it. And it is this theme in his thought that reflects many of the themes implicit in recent communitarian and postmodern thought; that is, theories that take seriously the social thesis in political theory but want to offer a normative critique of society (Taylor, 1989; Sandel, 1998). It is of little surprise that much of the communitarian strain in political thought was inspired by Charles Taylor (1931–), a thinker who owes more than a large debt to Hegel's work.

Hegel's impact on the debate between liberals and communitarians may yet be telling. He offers a metaphysical account of communitarianism (metaphysical in the way that Hobbes's *Leviathan* and Locke's *Second Treatise* were) that explains why it is necessary for the modern subject to feel at home in his community. The subject derives his or her identity from the existing moral fabric and its inherent values, and the modern subject needs to recognise these values as his or her own. Moreover, he prescribes normative constraints which determine which societies can formally and substantially meet the modern subject's need for reconciliation and, hence, why these are good societies. As for many communitarian writers, such 'rational' societies are not dissimilar to Western liberal states, but at least Hegel tells us a story of why this might be the case.

NOTES

CHAPTER 2

1   See Stern (2006). The best and most convincing account of the former position is Tugendhat (1986, chaps 13–14). A less sophisticated version, yet more famous, is of course Popper (1957, chaps 11–12). For the latter position, see Hardimon (1994), Neuhouser (2000), Patten (1999), the final chapter of Pippin (1997) and also Pippin (2000) and Williams (1997). There is also much interest in Hegel's contribution to contemporary debates in politics and ethics; see Knowles (2002) and Wood (1990).

CHAPTER 3

1   One needs to look at the introduction to the SL for Hegel's description of his own method.
2   The difference from Kant, and from the central current of the Enlightenment, is almost a refrain in Hegel's philosophy, and we shall return to it again and again, most notably in our discussion of moral freedom later in this book.
3   The contemporary heirs of which are often called communitarians. See Mulhall and Swift (1996) for an overview.
4   We return to this discussion in chapter 4, pp. 50–2.
5   In many ways, the left-Hegelians (see chapter 8 below) take this supposed conservatism as their point of departure from Hegel, most famously expressed by Marx: 'The philosophers have only interpreted the world, in various ways; the point is to change it' (Marx, 1977a, 158).
6   See Stern (2006). Stern himself offers a further 'neutral' reading. For a full discussion and further references, see parts 1 and 2 of Stewart (1996).

CHAPTER 4

1   Examples include Sartre (1965); Camus (2000); Bataille (1989); and Trocchi (1999).

2 I develop these themes in the next chapter; see especially pp. 58–63.

3 Hegel elsewhere states: 'I am free . . . when my existence depends on myself' (VPG, 17).

4 And this is why Hegel cannot adopt the social contract model of political obligation because that, at base, relies on immutable human nature and not the idea of perfectionism.

5 For the relationship between Hegel and Rousseau, see Neuhouser (2000).

6 This is another sense in which one can understand Hegel's enigmatic aphorism: 'What is rational is actual; and what is actual is rational' (20). The following discussion of subjective and objective freedom owes a lot to Patten (1999) and Neuhouser (2000).

7 The objective will grounds Knowles's claim that the normative life of a society is a complex structure of will. And since the will is free, then these normative structures are just, legitimate and true when they are structures of freedom. We can only act freely in the context of a social life that maintains and promotes freedom. See Knowles (2002).

8 See Chapter 5 below.

9 A law is not a piece of paper. It is a mental phenomenon and social institutions are interpersonal structures of understandings, intentions and expectations objectified systematically in patterns of behaviour' (Knowles, 2002, 14).

CHAPTER 5

1 Do not confuse the grammatical use of 'subject' here with the moral subject which is the topic of the next chapter.

2 See Chapter 3, pp. 23–8.

3 The need to discuss recognition at this juncture in the argument is to be found in Hegel's own references in §§35R and 57R. For the rejection of social contract theory, see §§75 and 100R. See also Knowles (2002, 91–3); Wood (1990, 77–83); Williams (1997, 31–3) and Pippin (2000).

4 Hegel states that 'persons' first appear around AD 300 under Roman law and, to give you an idea of the pace of historical development, it takes another 1500 years before the institution of private property is recognised as the rational embodiment of personality. See §34, 35, 57 and 62.

5 There is more to say on this point. The state can execute criminals and conscript individuals into the armed forces, but Hegel could tell a story about how these practices can be justified by freedom as well.

6 Some objects cannot be alienated, only those things which are 'external' in nature. Hegel lists life, free will and conscience. The idea being I cannot alienate those things that will lead to a violation of freedom if freedom is the justification of the rights in the first place. See §§65 and 66.

7 See the similar account in Locke (1988, ¶¶7–13, 312–17).

CHAPTER 6

1 Such necessity is called for when an agent's actions continually contradict avowed intentions, as would be the case with neurotic symptoms, for example.

2 Obviously, in terms of *Sittlichkeit*, this shared scheme of interpretation will demand more. For Hegel's account as a whole, a demonstration of the logical unity of *Sittlichkeit* and objective freedom – in that it enables satisfaction of subjective freedom for the subject who inhabits the rational state and not just any form of life – is necessary. At this point, though, the concern is merely with morality and the harmonisation of the agent's intention with the other's interpretation of it, and, as such, it need only rely on a shared set of values, meanings and significations as concerns action. *Sittlichkeit* is the subject of the next chapter.

3 Hegel's reading of Kant and the subsequent literature is vast. I am going to introduce only what is necessary to understand Hegel's argument much to the detriment of a proper evaluation of Kant's own ethics. For the substantial debate, the reader should begin with Allision (1990, chap. 10); Korsgaard (1996, chap. 3); O'Neill (1989, part 2); O'Hagan (1987); Pippin (1997, part 1); and Wood (1989).

4 See chapter 3, pp. 21–2.

5 Probably the most influential work in contemporary ethics, Rawls (1972), begins from this very premise.

6 See fn. 3 above for further reading.

7 Of course, this is only the first formulation of the categorical imperative, but it seems to suffer the brunt of Hegel's challenges. The second formulation of the categorical imperative – '. . . all rational beings stand under the *law* that each of them is to treat himself and all others *never merely as means* but *always at the same time as ends in themselves*' (Kant, 1997, 41) – has offered contemporary writers much more scope to construct a viable Kantian ethics. See, for example, Korsgaard (1996) and O'Neill (1989).

CHAPTER 7

1 I have used the term ethical life throughout the book without any overt definition. My action was deliberate. I have also used 'way' or 'form of life' and 'moral' and 'social fabric' interchangeably with ethical life and shall continue to do so. One could also use 'tradition' or 'community'. As a preference, I think that the English expression of 'moral fabric' is probably closest to the German *Sittlichkeit*. Some of the alternative terms have different emphases, however. For example, form of life refers to those explicit conditions which govern one's practical reasoning; whereas tradition has more to do with the historical origins and foundation of these conditions; community to one's immediate allegiance to a way of life; whereas *Sittlichkeit* (ethical substance or life) refers to all three aspects at once.

2 The structures of ethical life are objective in two ways: one, they exist independently of individuals in that you can change the members without changing the structures (there is a continuous body of Aston Villa fans even if those who constituted it originally in 1879 are no longer alive; the individual fans are 'accidental' to the existence of an organised fan base in Hegel's term (§§144–5)); and two, they can be known by agents and hence the subject of true and false judgements (§146).

3 Contemporary adherents of the social thesis include Taylor (1989); MacIntyre (1988); Sandel (1998); and Walzer (1983). A good overview of these positions is Mulhall and Swift (1996).

4 'Man is a bearer of private rights because he is essentially a vehicle of rational will.' (Taylor, 1975, 428).

5 See pp. 134–6.

6 'The family introduces man to community – to the relation of interdependence in society; and this union is a moral one . . .' (VPG, 422).

7 For one example, see the usage of 'civil society' in chapter 8 of Locke (1988).

8 Marx's critique of Hegel is most pertinent when he shifts his attack from metaphysics to the actual workings of the capitalist system and private property. The claim is that capitalism and private property obstruct freedom and self-determination. See Marx (1977b).

9 Note that the estates are not Marx's classes – they are 'vertical' not 'horizontal': the agricultural landowners, peasants and farmer managers all belong to one; the factory workers, factory owners and foremen belong to another. See Knowles (2002, 270–1).

10 Hegel uses the term 'state' in two distinct ways: one, 'the *political* state proper and its constitution' (§267), that is, the political and social institutions which control civil society; two, he refers to the rational whole of a people determined by a common ethical life which includes all those independent moments such as the abstract person, the family, civil society, *et al.* For a discussion of Hegel's use of 'state' see Pelczynski (1971a).

11 Although, when the social bonds of a nation are weakened, Hegel does prescribe a jolly good war to strengthen the national spirit (§324). Now, the World Cup probably serves the same function.

12 '. . . there is something in the nature of a rational social order that makes it difficult, or even impossible, to know what the character of that order would be unless it had been instantiated somewhere in practice' (Patten, 1999, 15–16).

13 For the full story, the next text by Hegel the reader ought to pick up is VPG.

NOTES FOR FURTHER READING

WORKS OF HEGEL

The collected works of Hegel is published in 21 volumes as *Hegel: Werke*, ed. Moldenhauer, E. and Michel, K. Frankfurt am Main: Suhrkamp, 1986 (c. 1969–79). Below I list a selection of his major works in chronological order by date of approximate composition:

1802/3   *On the Scientific Ways of Treating Natural Law, on its Place in Moral Philosophy, and its Relation to the Positive Sciences of Right*, trans. Nisbet, H. in *Political Writings*. Cambridge: Cambridge University Press, 1999.

1803/4   *System of Ethical Life*, trans. Knox, T. and Harris, H.; and *First Philosophy of Spirit*, trans. Harris, H. New York: State University of New York Press, 1979 (published together in one volume).

1807   *The Phenomenology of Spirit*, trans. Miller, A. Oxford: Oxford University Press, 1977.

1812–16   *Science of Logic*, trans. Miller, A. New York: Humanity Books, 1999.

1817/18   *Lectures on Natural Right and Political Science: The First Philosophy of Right*, trans. Stewart, J. and Hodgson, P. London: University of California Press, 1995.

1821   *Elements of the Philosophy of Right*, trans. Nisbet, H. Cambridge: Cambridge University Press, 1991; also available as *Hegel's Philosophy of Right*, trans. Knox, T. Oxford: Oxford University Press, 1967; and *Philosophy of Right*, trans. Dyde, S. Ontario, Canada: Batoche Books, 2001.

1822   *Philosophy of History*, trans. Sibree, J. New York: Prometheus Books, 1991.

1830   *The Encyclopaedia Logic: Part 1 of the Encyclopaedia of Philosophical Sciences with the Zusätze*, trans. Geraets, T., Suchting, A. and Harris, H. Indianapolis, USA: Hackett Publishing Co., 1991.

1830   *Hegel's Philosophy of Nature: Part 2 of the Encylopaedia of the Philosophical Sciences*, trans. Miller, A. Oxford: Oxford University Press, 2004.

1830   *Philosophy of Mind: Part 3 of the Encyclopaedia of Philosophical Sciences with the Zusätze*, trans. Wallace, W. and Miller, A. Oxford: Oxford University Press, 1971.

FURTHER READING ON HEGEL'S PHILOSOPHY

I here list the books that I believe would constitute the next step if the reader were interested in deepening his or her understanding of Hegel's philosophy in general or his social philosophy in particular.

Hegel's philosophy in general

For a general introduction to Hegel's philosophy as a whole, I would recommend the comprehensive and ambitious work by Taylor (1975). If that is too daunting, the author very kindly reduced it to a more accessible version predominantly concerned with Hegel's political thought: Taylor (1979). More accessible still is Singer's little book (2001) which ought to get a novice started. For a narration of Hegel's life interspersed with critical comments, see Pinkard (2000). Useful collections of articles include Beiser (1993), Inwood (1985), Lamb (1998), MacIntyre (1972) and Priest (1987). A useful resource is the Hegelian dictionary compiled by Inwood (1992).

Hegel's ethical and social thought

Two good introductions which relate Hegel to concerns in contemporary political thought and ethics are Knowles (2002) and Wood (1990). For more contextual and interpretative approaches, see Avineri (1972), Hardimon (1994) and Houlgate (1991). For more advanced studies, see Neuhouser (2000), Patten (1999) and Williams

(1997). A good collection of articles concerned solely with the political aspect of Hegel's thought is Pelczynski (1971).

SELECTIVE BIBLIOGRAPHY

Allison, H. (1990), *Kant's Theory of Freedom*, Cambridge: Cambridge University Press.

Aristotle (1996), *The Politics*, trans. Jowett, B. in *The Politics and the Constitution of Athens*, ed. Everson, S., Cambridge: Cambridge University Press

Avineri, S. (1972), *Hegel's Theory of the Modern State*, Cambridge: Cambridge University Press.

Bataille, G. (1989), *L'Abbé C*, trans. Facey, P., London: Marion Boyars.

Beauvoir, S. de (1997), *The Second Sex*, trans. and ed. Parshley, H., London: Vintage Classics.

Beiser, F. (ed.) (1993), *The Cambridge Companion to Hegel*, Cambridge: Cambridge University Press.

Camus, A. (2000), *The Outsider*, trans. Laredo, J., London: Penguin.

Ceram, C. (2001), *Gods, Graves and Scholars: The story of archaeology*, London: Phoenix Books.

Descartes, R. (1996), *Meditations on First Philosophy*, ed. Cottingham, J., Cambridge: Cambridge University Press.

Filmer, R. (1991), *'Patriarcha' and Other Writings*, Cambridge: Cambridge University Press.

Frankfurt, H. (1982), 'Freedom of the Will and the Concept of a Person', in Watson (1982).

Hardimon, M. (1994), *Hegel's Social Philosophy: The Project of Reconciliation*, Cambridge: Cambridge University Press.

Herodotus (1936), *The History of Herodotus*, trans. Rawlinson, G., New York: Tudor Publishing Company.

Hobbes, T. (1982), *Leviathan*, London: Penguin.

Houlgate, S. (1991), *Freedom, Truth and History*, London: Routledge.

—— (1992), 'Hegel's Ethical Thought', *Bulletin of the Hegel Society of Great Britain*, 25, 1–17.

Hume, D. (1962), *A Treatise on Human Nature*, vol. 2., London: J. M. Dent & Son.

Hyppolite, J. (1974), *Genesis and Structure of Hegel's Phenomenology of Spirit*, Evanston, USA: Northwestern University Press.

Inwood, M. (ed.) (1985), *Hegel*, Oxford: Oxford University Press.

—— (1992), *A Hegel Dictionary*, Oxford: Blackwell.

Kant, I. (1991), 'An Answer to the Question: What is Enlightenment?', in Kant, *Political Writings*, ed. Reiss, H., Cambridge: Cambridge University Press.

—— (1993), *Critique of Pure Reason*, trans. Meiklejohn, J. (revised by Politis, V.), London: Everyman.

—— (1997), *Groundwork for the Metaphysics of Morals*, trans. Gregor, M., Cambridge: Cambridge University Press.

Knowles, D. (1998), 'Hegel on Will, Freedom and Right', in Lamb (1998, vol. 1).

Knowles, D. (2002), *Hegel and the Philosophy of Right*, London: Routledge.
Kojève, A. (1969), *Introduction to the Reading of Hegel*, 2nd edn, trans. Nichols, J., London: Basic Books Inc.
Korsgaard, C. (1996), *Creating the Kingdom of End*, Cambridge: Cambridge University Press.
Lamb, D. (ed.) (1998), *Hegel*, 2 vols, Aldershot: Ashgate/Dartmouth.
Locke, J. (1988), *Second Treatise on Government*, in *Two Treatises of Government*, Cambridge: Cambridge University Press.
MacIntyre, A. (ed.) (1972), *Hegel: A Collection of Critical Essays*, London: University of Notre Dame Press.
—— (1988), *Whose Justice? Which Rationality?*, London: Duckworth.
Marx, K. (1977), *Selected Writings*, ed. McLellan, D., Oxford: Oxford University Press.
—— (1977a), *Theses on Feuerbach*, in Marx (1977).
—— (1977b), *Critique of Hegel's 'Philosophy of Right'*, in Marx (1977).
—— (1977c), *The German Ideology*, in Marx (1977).
—— (1977d), 'Preface to *A Contribution to the Critique of Political Economy*', in Marx (1977).
Mulhall, S. and Swift, A. (1996), *Liberals and Communitarians*, 2nd edn, Oxford: Blackwell.
Neuhouser, F. (2000), *Foundations of Hegel's Social Theory: Actualizing Freedom*, London: Harvard University Press.
O'Hagan, T. (1987), 'On Hegel's Critique of Kant's Moral and Political Philosophy', in Priest (1987).
O'Neill, O. (1989), *Constructions of Reason: Explorations of Kant's Practical Philosophy*, Cambridge: Cambridge University Press.
Patten, A. (1999), *Hegel's Idea of Freedom*, Oxford: Oxford University Press.
Pelczynski, Z. (ed.) (1971), *Hegel's Political Philosophy: Problems and Perspectives*, Cambridge: Cambridge University Press.
—— (1971a), 'The Hegelian Conception of the State', in Pelczynski (1971).
Pinkard, T. (2000), *Hegel: A biography*, Cambridge: Cambridge University Press.
Pippin, R. (1997), *Idealism as Modernism: Hegelian Variations*, Cambridge: Cambridge University Press.
—— (2000), 'What is the Question for which Hegel's Theory of Recognition is the Answer?', *European Journal of Philosophy*, 8, (2), 155–72.
Popper, K. (1957), *The Open Society and its Enemies*, vol. 2, 3rd edn, London: Routledge.
Priest, S. (ed.) (1987), *Hegel's Critique of Kant*, Oxford: Clarendon.
Rawls, J. (1972), *A Theory of Justice*, Oxford: Clarendon Press.
Rousseau, J.-J. (1997), *The Social Contract*, trans. Gourevitch, V. in *The Social Contract and Other Later Political Writings*, Cambridge: Cambridge University Press.
Sandel, M. (1998), *Liberalism and the Limits of Justice*, Cambridge: Cambridge University Press.
Sartre, J.-P. (1965), *Nausea*, trans. Baldick, R., London: Penguin.
—— (1989), *Being and Nothingness*, trans. Barnes, H., London: Routledge.

Sartre, J.-P. (1991), *The Critique of Dialectical Reason*, vol. 1., trans. Sheridan-Smith, A., London: Verso.

—— (1992), *Notebooks for an Ethics*, trans. Pellauer, D., London: University of Chicago Press.

Singer, P. (2001), *Hegel: A very short introduction*, Oxford: Oxford University Press.

—— (2002), 'All Animals are Equal', in *Unsanctifying Human Life*, ed. Kuhse, H., Oxford: Blackwell.

Stern, R. (2006), 'Hegel's *Doppelsatz*: A neutral reading', *Journal of the History of Philosophy*, 44, (2), 235–66.

Stewart, J. (ed.) (1996), *The Hegel Myths and Legends*, Evanston, USA: Northwestern University Press.

Taylor, C. (1975), *Hegel*, Cambridge: Cambridge University Press.

—— (1977), 'What is Human Agency?', in *The Self: Psychological and Philosophical Issues*, ed. Mischel, T., Oxford: Blackwell.

—— (1979), *Hegel and Modern Society*, Cambridge: Cambridge University Press.

—— (1982), 'Responsibility for Self', in Watson (1982).

—— (1989), *Sources of the Self*, Cambridge: Cambridge University Press.

Trocchi, A. (1999), *Young Adam*, Edinburgh: Rebel Inc.

Tugendhat, E. (1986), *Self-consciousness and Self-determination*, trans. Stern, P., London: MIT Press.

Walzer, M. (1983), *Spheres of Justice*, New York: Basic Books.

Watson, G. (ed.) (1982), *Free Will*, Oxford: Oxford University Press.

Williams, R. (1997), *Hegel's Ethics of Recognition*, London: University of California Press.

Wolf, S. (1990), *Freedom within Reason*, Oxford: Oxford University Press.

Wood, A. (1989), 'The Emptiness of the Moral Will', *Monist*, 72, 454–83.

—— (1990), *Hegel's Ethical Thought*, Cambridge: Cambridge University Press.

—— (1992), 'Reply', *Bulletin of the Hegel Society of Great Britain*, 25, 34–50.

INDEX